AF789707

LAW, CRIME AND LAW ENFORCEMENT

EXONERATED BY DNA

ISSUES AND CASE PROFILES IN THE USE OF EXCULPATORY DNA EVIDENCE

LAW, CRIME AND LAW ENFORCEMENT

Additional books in this series can be found on Nova's website
under the Series tab.

Additional e-books in this series can be found on Nova's website
under the e-book tab.

LAW, CRIME AND LAW ENFORCEMENT

EXONERATED BY DNA

ISSUES AND CASE PROFILES IN THE USE OF EXCULPATORY DNA EVIDENCE

DARRELL SHAW
EDITOR

nova publishers
New York

Copyright © 2015 by Nova Science Publishers, Inc.

All rights reserved. No part of this book may be reproduced, stored in a retrieval system or transmitted in any form or by any means: electronic, electrostatic, magnetic, tape, mechanical photocopying, recording or otherwise without the written permission of the Publisher.

For permission to use material from this book please contact us:
Telephone 631-231-7269; Fax 631-231-8175
Web Site: http://www.novapublishers.com

NOTICE TO THE READER

The Publisher has taken reasonable care in the preparation of this book, but makes no expressed or implied warranty of any kind and assumes no responsibility for any errors or omissions. No liability is assumed for incidental or consequential damages in connection with or arising out of information contained in this book. The Publisher shall not be liable for any special, consequential, or exemplary damages resulting, in whole or in part, from the readers' use of, or reliance upon, this material. Any parts of this book based on government reports are so indicated and copyright is claimed for those parts to the extent applicable to compilations of such works.

Independent verification should be sought for any data, advice or recommendations contained in this book. In addition, no responsibility is assumed by the publisher for any injury and/or damage to persons or property arising from any methods, products, instructions, ideas or otherwise contained in this publication.

This publication is designed to provide accurate and authoritative information with regard to the subject matter covered herein. It is sold with the clear understanding that the Publisher is not engaged in rendering legal or any other professional services. If legal or any other expert assistance is required, the services of a competent person should be sought. FROM A DECLARATION OF PARTICIPANTS JOINTLY ADOPTED BY A COMMITTEE OF THE AMERICAN BAR ASSOCIATION AND A COMMITTEE OF PUBLISHERS.

Additional color graphics may be available in the e-book version of this book.

Library of Congress Cataloging-in-Publication Data

ISBN: 978-1-63463-963-7

Published by Nova Science Publishers, Inc. † New York

CONTENTS

PREFACE

Chapter 1 – DNA evidence offers prosecutors an important tool in the identification and apprehension of violent criminals, particularly in sexual assault cases. At the same time, DNA evidence can be used to exonerate the innocent. By highlighting the importance and utility of DNA evidence, this book presents challenges to the scientific and criminal justice communities. These challenges involve maintaining high standards for collecting and preserving DNA evidence, ensuring that DNA testing methodologies meet rigorous scientific criteria for reliability and accuracy, and increasing the proficiency and credibility of forensic scientists so their results and testimony are of the highest caliber, able to withstand exacting scrutiny. Commentaries and profiles of DNA exculpatory cases are presented to illustrate the power and potential of DNA evidence. Policy implications of DNA testing and use as evidence are also discussed.

Chapter 2 – Deoxyribonucleic acid, or DNA, is the fundamental building block for an individual's entire genetic makeup. DNA is a powerful tool for law enforcement investigations because each person's DNA is different from that of every other individual (except for identical twins). By analyzing selected DNA sequences (called loci), a crime laboratory can develop a profile to be used in identifying a suspect

This report provides an overview of how DNA is used to investigate crimes and help protect the innocent. It also reviews current statutory law on collecting DNA samples, sharing DNA profiles generated from those samples, and providing access to post-conviction DNA testing. The report also includes a summary of grant programs authorized by Congress to assist state and local governments with reducing DNA backlogs, provide post-conviction DNA testing, and promote new technology in the field. It also reviews select issues Congress might consider should it legislate or conduct oversight in this area.

In: Exonerated by DNA
Editor: Darrell Shaw
ISBN: 978-1-63463-963-7
© 2015 Nova Science Publishers, Inc.

Chapter 1

CONVICTED BY JURIES, EXONERATED BY SCIENCE: CASE STUDIES IN THE USE OF DNA EVIDENCE TO ESTABLISH INNOCENCE AFTER TRIAL*

Edward Connors, Thomas Lundregan,
Neal Miller and Tom McEwen

MESSAGE FROM THE ATTORNEY GENERAL

Our system of criminal justice is best described as a search for the truth. Increasingly, the forensic use of DNA technology is an important ally in that search. The development of DNA technology furthers the search for truth by helping police and prosecutors in the fight against violent crime. Through the use of DNA evidence, prosecutors are often able to conclusively establish the guilt of a defendant. Moreover, as some of the commentaries suggest, DNA evidence—like fingerprint evidence—offers prosecutors important new tools for the identification and apprehension of some of the most violent perpetrators, particularly in cases of sexual assault.

At the same time, DNA aids the search for truth by exonerating the innocent. The criminal justice system is not infallible, and this report documents

---

* This is an edited, reformatted and augmented version of research report, NCJ 161258, issued by the National Institute of Justice, June 1996.

cases in which the search for truth took a tortuous path. With the exception of one young man of limited mental capacity, who pleaded guilty, the individuals whose stories are told in the report were convicted after jury trials and were sentenced to long prison terms. They successfully challenged their convictions, using DNA tests on existing evidence. They had served, on average, 7 years in prison.

By highlighting the importance and utility of DNA evidence, this report presents challenges to the scientific and justice communities. Among the tasks ahead are the following: maintaining the highest standards for the collection and preservation of DNA evidence; ensuring that the DNA testing methodology meets rigorous scientific criteria for reliability and accuracy; and ensuring proficiency and credibility of forensic scientists so that their results and testimony are of the highest caliber and are capable of withstanding exacting scrutiny. Meeting these scientific challenges requires continued support for research that contributes to the advancement of the forensic sciences. The research agenda must also enable criminal justice practitioners to understand and to make appropriate use of the rapidly advancing and increasingly available technology. The National Institute of Justice (NIJ) commissioned this study to encourage discussion of the challenges to the scientific and justice communities presented by DNA evidence. The commentaries presented here—authored by prominent experts from a variety of disciplines—and the cases documented in the pages that follow, are testimony to the power and potential of DNA evidence. We hope that these commentaries and the NIJ report spur a broader debate about the value of DNA technology and the role of science in the criminal justice system's search for truth.

Janet Reno

FOREWORD: COMMENTARIES ON DNA TESTING

Commentary by Edward J. Imwinkelried
Professor of Law
University of California at Davis

The outcomes in the 28 cases documented in this report dramatize the real nature of the question of standards for determining the admissibility of scientific evidence in the United States.

Until recently, the *Frye* standard governed that question in most jurisdictions. In *Frye* v. *United States*,[1] the court announced that to be admissible, scientific testimony must be based on a technique that has "gained general acceptance in the particular field in which it belongs."[2] The court singled out novel scientific evidence and prescribed a special test for the introduction of such testimony. At one point, that test was the controlling law in both the Federal courts and 45 States.[3] It is true that in 1993 the United States Supreme Court abandoned *Frye* and adopted a more flexible validation standard in *Daubert* v. *Merrell Dow Pharmaceuticals, Inc.*[4] However, the Court decided *Daubert* on statutory rather than constitutional grounds, and, consequently, each State remains free to fashion its own standard for admitting scientific evidence. As of 1995, 22 States apparently remained committed to *Frye*.[5] In short, the conservative general acceptance test is still in place in almost half the States.

Moreover, even in his lead opinion in *Daubert*, Mr. Justice Blackmun indicated that, at least in some respects, trial judges may continue to admit scientific evidence more cautiously and restrictively. The Justice initially pointed to Federal Rule of Evidence 403, authorizing trial judges to exclude logically relevant evidence when "its probative value is substantially out-weighed by the danger of unfair prejudice, confusion of the issues, or misleading the jury...." The Justice then quoted Judge Weinstein, a distinguished jurist and scholar, as declaring: "[E]xpert evidence can be both powerful and quite misleading because of the difficulty in evaluating it. Because of this risk, the judge in weighing possible prejudice against probative force under Rule 403...exercises more control over experts than over lay witnesses."[6]

Two points must be made. First, Justice Blackmun and Judge Weinstein are voicing conventional wisdom in suggesting that lay jurors attach greater weight to scientific evidence. The California Supreme Court has asserted that a "misleading aura of certainty...often envelops a new scientific process."[7] In a similar vein, the Court of Appeals for the District of Columbia, birthplace of

---

[1] 293 F.1013 (D.C. Cir. 1923).

[2] Id. at 1014.

[3] Note, 40 *OHIO ST.L.J.* 757, 769 (1979).

[4] 113 S.Ct. 2786 (1993).

[5] Meaney, Joseph R., "From *Frye* to *Daubert*: Is a Pattern Unfolding?" 35 *JURIMETRICS* 191, 193 (1994).

[6] 138 *F.R.D.* at 632.

[7] *People* v. *Kelly*. 17 Cal. 3d 24, 32, 549 P.2d 1240, 1245, 130 *Cal. Rptr.* 144, 149 (1976).

the *Frye* rule, has written that jurors frequently attribute a "mystic infallibility" to scientific testimony.[8]

There have been empirical investigations into the impact that scientific evidence has on lay jurors. Although those studies are far from conclusive, they largely contradict the assertion that scientific evidence overwhelms lay jurors.[9] After surveying the literature, two respected commentators concluded that "the image of a spellbound jury mesmerized by...a forensic expert is more likely to reflect...fantasies than the...realities of courtroom testimony."[10]

Second, and more importantly, the advocates of special restrictions on the admissibility of scientific testimony misunderstand the fundamental nature of the question:

> It is misleading to focus solely on the strengths and weaknesses of scientific evidence. In principle, the judgment must be comparative. To the extent that we discriminate against scientific evidence, subjecting it to uniquely discriminatory, restrictive rules such as *Frye*, we encourage the courts to rely on other types of evidence. Thus, our task is not to make an absolute judgment about the merits of scientific evidence. Rather, our task is to compare it with other types of evidence to decide whether the differential treatment of scientific evidence is justifiable.[11]

As the 28 cases collected in this report demonstrate, when we subject new scientific techniques such as DNA typing to special admissibility rules, we force the courts to rely on inferior types of evidence, such as eyewitness testimony. In all 28 cases, without the benefit of DNA evidence, the triers of fact had to rely on eyewitness testimony, which turned out to be inaccurate. In *United States* v. *Wade*,[12] Mr. Justice Brennan noted: "The vagaries of eyewitness identification are well known; the annals of criminal law are rife with instances of mistaken identification." Those annals must now be lengthened to include the 28 wrongful convictions discussed in this report. In roughly two-thirds of the cases, the triers heard testimony based on traditional forms of expertise, such as hair analysis—testimony that passes muster under the *Frye* standard but that, again, turned out to be erroneous. There are numerous

[8] *United States* v. *Addison*, 498 F.2d 741, 744 (D.C. Cir. 1974).

[9] "Standard for Admitting Scientific Evidence: A Critique from the Perspective of Juror Psychology," 28 *VILL.L.REV.* 554 (1983) 566–70.

[10] Rogers, Richard, and Charles Patrick Ewing, "Ultimate Opinion Prescriptions: A Cosmetic Fix and a Plea for Empiricism," 13 LAW 7 *HUM.BEHAV.* 357, 363 (1989).

[11] 28 *VILL.L.REV.* at 564.

[12] 388 U.S. 218 (1967).

proficiency studies establishing that there is a significant margin of error in such traditional forensic techniques.[13] The sobering fact is that in all 28 cases, the error was unmasked—and justice finally served—only because of the novel scientific technique of DNA typing.

The "junk science" controversy has made it tempting to propose special restrictions for scientific evidence, especially testimony resting on relatively new scientific techniques. One lesson to be learned from this report, however, is that before succumbing to that temptation, we should pause to pose two questions. First, have the critics of scientific evidence *proven* that the type of testimony in question presents a unique probative danger—or have they merely made that assertion? Further, if we impose a unique restriction on scientific testimony, on balance are the courts more likely to reach just results—or are we condemning the courts to reliance on suspect types of testimony that call into question the caliber of justice dispensed in our courts? This report should be read with those two questions foremost in mind.

Commentary by Walter F. Rowe
Professor, Department of Forensic Sciences
The George Washington University

The introduction of DNA profiling has revolutionized forensic science and the criminal justice system. DNA technology has given police and the courts a means of identifying the perpetrators of rapes and murders with a very high degree of confidence.

As recently as the late 1960s, the only methods available for genetic marker analysis of blood and other body fluids were the Lattes test, the absorption-elution test, and the absorption-inhibition test. Only ABO blood group substances and ABO isoantibodies could be detected in biological stain evidence. Over the intervening years, electrophoretic methods for typing polymorphic proteins—such as phosphoglucomutase, esterase D, glyoxalase, hemoglobin, and haptoglobin—became available.

While these methods are in theory capable of greatly narrowing down the possible sources of biological stain evidence, they often fail to yield a result because of deterioration of the genetic marker. They even can yield completely erroneous results.

[13] Giannelli, Paul C., "The Admissibility of Laboratory Reports: The Reliability of Scientific Proof," 49 *OHIO ST.L.J.* 671 (1988).

For a variety of reasons, DNA profiling has significantly advanced the analysis of biological stain evidence. First, these methods are intrinsically more discriminating than the methods of genetic marker analysis heretofore used. DNA profiling is more likely to exonerate a wrongly accused suspect. Second, the DNA molecule is more stable than polymorphic proteins. Third, microbial degradation does not lead to erroneous typing results.

An unforeseen consequence of the introduction of DNA profiling has been the reopening of old cases. Persons convicted of murder and rape before DNA profiling became available have sought to have the evidence in their cases reevaluated using this new technology. In some cases, DNA test results have exonerated those convicted of the offenses and resulted in their release from prison.

The National Institute of Justice commissioned a research study of such DNA exculpatory cases. Conducted by the Institute for Law and Justice and described in this report, the study has identified 28 cases in which DNA testing led to the exoneration of persons previously convicted of murder or rape.

Most forensic scientists involved in DNA analysis have been aware that in some cases, DNA profiling has been instrumental in correcting injustices. Previously, however, almost all the information had been anecdotal. This report assembles a wealth of information on such cases, and the accounts of exculpatory DNA cases it presents will go a long way toward countering uninformed attacks on forensic DNA testing. Study results also should provide strong arguments for law enforcement officials who seek funding from State legislatures to establish forensic DNA laboratories. Furthermore, the study should completely dispel any lingering public perception of forensic DNA testing as a threat to civil liberties.

At the same time, the study also raises several important issues that need to be confronted by the legal community, law enforcement agencies, and the forensic science profession. The careful reader of this report will note the number of cases in which law enforcement agencies and prosecutors went forward with criminal prosecutions when only minimal genetic marker data were available. Critics of DNA typing who have opposed the admission of any DNA evidence should ponder the likely consequences of such an absolute prohibition: Law enforcement agencies and forensic science laboratories would be compelled to revert to the older and less discriminating serological methods (such as ABO blood typing and polymorphic protein typing). Many innocent defendants who would be exonerated by DNA typing would instead be prosecuted because the less powerful techniques failed to exclude them.

A second important issue is the number of cases in which there was misconduct on the part of the prosecution's scientific experts. For example, the forensic serologist who testified against Gary Dotson failed to disclose that, because the alleged victim was also a type B secretor, the fraction of the male population that could have contributed the semen found on the vaginal swabs exceeded 60 percent, making the serological evidence in the case probative of very little.[14] In this instance, the prosecution's expert witness failed to volunteer potentially exculpatory information but did not actually lie under oath.

Three cases discussed in this report involved expert scientific testimony by Fred Zain. Mr. Zain was a forensic serologist in the West Virginia State Police Crime Laboratory for a number of years; he then worked briefly as a forensic serologist for the Bexar County (Texas) Medical Examiner's Office. Mr. Zain's conduct as a forensic serologist was called into question when the results of a DNA test freed Glen Woodall. At Mr. Woodall's original trial, Zain testified that Woodall's ABO, phosphoglucomutase (PGM), glyoxalase (GLO), and secretor types matched those found in the semen sample. Such an event is possible but highly unlikely given that Woodall was unambiguously excluded by subsequent DNA tests. A special commission convened by order of the West Virginia Supreme Court of Appeals investigated Zain and the West Virginia State Police Crime Laboratory. As a result of this investigation, the State Supreme Court ruled that none of the testimony given by Zain in more than 130 cases was credible.[15] The court further ordered that Zain be indicted for perjury.[16] It is sobering to reflect that but for the adventitious appearance of DNA typing, Glen Woodall would still be languishing in prison and Fred Zain might still be sending innocent persons to prison.

The advent of DNA typing will go a long way toward preventing miscarriages of justice, like the Dotson and Woodall cases, in the future. Most wrongly accused suspects will be exonerated during the initial testing of physical evidence, long before prosecution would even be considered. The quantity and quality of documentation required by laboratory quality assurance/quality control protocols preclude the wholesale falsification of test results. The minuscule quantities of DNA required for PCR-based typing

---

[14] Webb, Cathleen Crowell, and Marie Chapian, *Forgive Me*, New York: Berkeley Books, 1986.

[15] "Court Invalidates a Decade of Blood Test Results in Criminal Cases," *New York Times* (November 12, 1993):A20.

[16] Harper, Jane, "West Virginia Court Wants Forensics Expert Prosecuted," *Houston Post* (July 17, 1994):A22.

procedures also allow the preservation of sufficient DNA for independent laboratory testing.

One problem that DNA testing will not remedy is inadequate legal counsel. In case after case reported here, defense counsel failed to consult competent scientific experts. Even a neophyte forensic serologist would have detected the problems with the prosecution's serological evidence in the Dotson case. It is also clear that in case after case, defense counsel failed to review the case notes of the prosecution's forensic serologists. Even a layperson would have seen that Fred Zain's written reports and sworn testimony were contradicted by his case notes. Again, one has to reflect on the likelihood that numerous innocent persons are presently incarcerated because of the inadequacy of their attorneys.

This National Institute of Justice report on DNA exculpatory cases is a unique contribution to the growing literature on forensic DNA profiling. It should be read and pondered by anyone having an interest in this burgeoning field of forensic science.

Commentary by Rockne Harmon
Senior Deputy District Attorney Alameda County, California

The introduction of forensic DNA typing into the legal system was heralded as the most significant event in criminalistics since dermal fingerprint identification. Few developments ever live up to their advance billing—but DNA has!

Cases are now being prosecuted that never would have been possible before the advent of DNA typing. Many States have created DNA data bases on known offenders that they compare against unsolved crimes. Several States have produced matches from their data base searches, and a handful of these cases already have been successfully prosecuted.

About 9 years after its introduction, forensic DNA typing is still used only selectively. This is due, in part, to several factors: the unavailability of forensic typing to local prosecutors, the time required to perform the typing, and the costs of the tests if private laboratories are utilized.

When forensic DNA typing is performed in cases under investigation or still pending in court, the results occasionally exonerate a suspect or suspects. Such cases rarely are front-page news because the tests have served their purpose. Investigators can redirect their efforts to alternative suspects. Prosecutors can dismiss charges filed against innocent suspects.

This report reviews more than two dozen cases in which forensic DNA typing ultimately exonerated suspects or defendants. Most were prosecuted at a time when forensic DNA typing was not available to police or prosecutors. Each case has a slightly different sequence and series of events. Because of these differences, each case provides additional insight into how the legal system might avoid the pitfalls of the past, whether or not the testing is performed in pending or postconviction cases.

Some already have used the cases discussed in this report to argue that hundreds more innocent defendants are in prison. They contend that the current "exclusion" rate for forensic DNA labs—close to 25 percent—suggests that a similar percentage of innocent defendants were wrongly convicted before the availability of forensic DNA typing. Unfortunately, too many variables are contained in the "exclusion" rate to draw any meaningful conclusions from it. Furthermore, nothing about the cases reviewed here necessarily supports such a conclusion.

The only clear conclusion that can be drawn is that this new technology can be used within the existing legal framework to undo past injustices. In other words, both the science and the legal system worked in these cases! This report provides additional insights into how such cases can be identified in the future.

Commentary by Ronald S. Reinstein
Presiding Judge, Criminal Department
Superior Court of Arizona Maricopa County

This report is an excellent example of the marriage between science and law and of the invaluable resource that DNA evidence has become in the forensic field. When justice can be served in such dramatic fashion by the exoneration of previously adjudged guilty individuals, science demonstrates its practical effect.

Yet the 28 cases cited in the report relate only to individuals released from prison because of DNA testing. Vastly more far-reaching in the long run is the use of DNA typing both to exclude some suspects who otherwise might be charged and to identify many other suspects who might not have been charged but for the DNA typing.

What is frustrating to many who are excited about the possibilities of the use of DNA in the forensics area is the slow pace it is traveling on the road to admissibility. Many jurisdictions do not have sufficient funds to establish their own laboratories or to send to private laboratories items of evidence for typing. Laboratories that perform testing often have backlogs measured in months. Courts, prosecutors, and defense counsel impose a great burden on laboratories' time in the usual discovery battles that occur whenever a new technique arrives on the forensic scene.

It is interesting to observe how quickly some DNA-evidence opponents embrace the science when it benefits certain defendants' interests but how defensive they become when the evidence points *toward* other defendants. But this is not unique to DNA evidence.

It is the responsibility of the court to promote the search for truth. If that search can be assisted by science that can give reliable results, the whole system as well as society benefits. It is also the responsibility of the court to try to prevent juror confusion caused by lawyers and experts who sometimes seem unable to explain scientific evidence in language the jury understands.

The future should be brighter as the technology improves so that the process of DNA typing will likely become much quicker, less complex, and less expensive. The battle of the experts, it is hoped, will also subside eventually, especially in the confusing area of the statistical meaning of a match.

The conflict between various forensic experts, population geneticists, and statisticians on "the meaning of a match" is a prime example of how science and the law sometimes do not mesh, especially in jurisdictions that follow the *Frye* test of general acceptance in the scientific community. The numbers being bandied about by various experts are almost beyond comprehension for trial jurors.

It seems logical to allow relevant, reliable, qualitative expert opinion—for example, that the probability of a random match in DNA testing is extremely remote given a reliable multilocus match. Likewise, experts should be able to testify from their experience about whether they are aware of random matches at four or five loci of unrelated individuals, and whether one evidence sample matches another to a reasonable degree of scientific certainty. There is a serious question about whether DNA-match testimony should be treated any differently from that of fingerprints, bite marks, hair and fiber samples, ballistics, shoe prints, and the like.

Restrictions currently imposed in some jurisdictions on the use of DNA evidence unreasonably divest such evidence of its compelling nature. If our justice system's goal is the continuing search for truth, as evidenced by the results of the study described in this report, then a similar argument can be made for the admissibility of relevant and reliable DNA-match testimony in our courts.

Commentary by George W. Clarke and Catherine Stephenson Deputy District Attorneys San Diego County, California

The study described in this report highlights significant aspects of the use of DNA evidence in the investigation and prosecution of criminal cases. While DNA typing is employed in various types of criminal cases (e.g., murder, robbery, kidnaping), the majority of DNA investigations entail sexual assault offenses. Indeed, in all of the cases reported in this study, sexual assault was alleged alone or in tandem with other crimes.

That the majority of DNA profiling cases concern sexual assault—usually rape—is not surprising. In few other criminal endeavors is the perpetrator as likely to deposit significant physical evidence. Occasionally, that evidence is hair, blood, or saliva; more often it is semen. Of the 28 cases reported in this study, all but two appear to have involved the analysis of the sperm component of the semen. Sexual assault cases by their very nature normally include evidence rich in DNA profile evidence.

Our enthusiasm for the use and interpretation of DNA typing, however, should be tempered inasmuch as the vast majority of sexual assault cases involving both child and adult victims do not require resolution of identity. The majority of child and adult sexual assault cases presented to us for determinations of whether to file criminal charges involve a perpetrator known to the victim. The defense normally presented is consent. In other cases, there is a denial that any sexual act occurred at all. These cases frequently do not involve physical evidence of sexual assault (injury, semen, saliva). This absence of physical evidence can be due to delay on the part of the victim in making a report to the police or to the very nature of the act, such as fondling, which is unlikely to result in the deposit or recovery of trace evidence. In such cases, the prosecutor first must resolve whether an assault even took place.

This report emphasizes that in those cases where identity *is* an issue, law enforcement officers must be diligent in the search for DNA evidence both at the scene and in or on the victim. Careful and timely collection and preservation of evidentiary material is critical. Collecting the bed sheets before they are washed and recovering evidence from the victim before the victim showers are important components of effective investigation. Thorough, well-documented, and honestly disseminated interviews of the victim are equally critical.

Forensic DNA typing laboratories—as numerous commentators have noted—encounter rates of exclusion of suspected attackers in close to 25 percent of cases. Careful examination of such results is commonly required whether in the pre- or postconviction setting. Typing results that exclude a suspected assailant may not demonstrate innocence. Not uncommonly, evidence collected and subjected to DNA profiling may reveal results from biological material left by other consensual sexual partners unrelated to the offense investigated or from other individuals having contact with the victim. Consideration of those results in the context of all other evidence in a specific case is essential to the determination of what took place. Law enforcement officers, prosecutors, and judges must conscientiously undertake such examinations in order to fulfill the factfinding functions with which they are entrusted.

As this report notes, judges and juries may soon routinely expect DNA typing evidence in sexual assault cases as the use of DNA technology becomes more widely known. DNA profiling evidence can speak, but not with the passion of a victim's voice. DNA typing results can shed light on "who"; it cannot explain precisely when, or how, or even why. The victim who survives the sexual assault must always be the primary and most important source of information.

Commentary by Matt L. Rodriguez Superintendent of Police Chicago Police Department

Criminal justice in the United States is a system founded on skepticism. "Innocent until proven guilty" and "beyond reasonable doubt" reflect more than the systematic doubt and deferred judgment that are afforded individuals accused of crime in our society. These maxims help define the incredibly high standards that the system's practitioners must meet before someone can be judged guilty.

In recent years police and prosecutors have increasingly turned to technology as a way to achieve these standards of proof with greater efficiency and effectiveness. Throughout the Nation, law enforcement agencies have entered an era in which high technology is not only desirable but also necessary to combat crime and ensure justice. Recent advances in forensic and biometric technologies, in particular, have created enormous opportunities for law enforcement to identify offenders with greater speed and certainty.

But while new technology presents opportunities, it is not without its challenges. The rate of change in technology, already fast-paced, is accelerating rapidly. And the demands on law enforcement are increasing dramatically in terms of both case volume and complexity. This environment of change exerts tremendous pressure on today's law enforcement administrators. Not only must we figure out what new technology to acquire and when to acquire it, but, just as importantly, we must ensure that our internal policies and operational procedures are keeping pace with advances in technology.

This study of DNA analysis in exculpatory cases highlights—in a very "real world" manner—both the opportunities and the challenges that this particular technology poses for law enforcement.

As a forensic science tool for criminal justice, DNA analysis has a relatively short history, dating back to groundbreaking cases in the late 1980s. What is significant about this "start date," from a law enforcement perspective, is that it stands in stark contrast to the age and experience levels of many of our police officers, especially those in larger cities. With an average age oftentimes of 40 or more, and with many police officers having 15, 20, or more years of experience, police departments today are populated with officers who did not grow up with DNA analysis and similar technologies. The result is that many agencies are still playing "catch up" when it comes to operating in today's high-technology world.

At the same time, the O.J. Simpson case and other recent sensational trials have put law enforcement under an intensely powerful microscope, examining our most basic procedures for collecting, processing, and caring for evidence. Although such scrutiny is never comfortable, it is appropriate and welcome, for the ultimate test of what we do in policing is in the courtroom. Increased scrutiny has challenged police departments to become more knowledgeable about DNA technology and more professional in evidence collection and processing. How we respond to this challenge will be crucial to our success and to the cause of justice in an even higher tech future.

Typically, when faced with challenges of this magnitude, law enforcement's first reaction is to concentrate on the specialists within our profession—in this case, the evidence technicians and crime laboratory analysts. These people are certainly critical to the effective processing of evidence, especially in the current environment of scrutiny and technological sophistication. But it is a mistake for law enforcement to focus solely on these specialists. Extensive and up-to-date training and procedures need to be provided to all of our police officers.

As the first responders to most crime scenes, patrol officers in particular must be aware of the potential opportunities and pitfalls posed by DNA technology, just as they must be extremely sensitive to the full range of evidentiary matters involved in protecting and processing crime scenes. Up and down the chain of command as well, police personnel must become more knowledgeable about DNA technology and more aware of, and responsive to, its implications for crime-scene and evidence processing. In the postO.J. Simpson era, the handling of evidence until it reaches the crime laboratory will be as important as the laboratory technology, conditions, or procedures themselves.

Although the challenges posed by DNA analysis are many, they are outweighed by the enormous possibilities the technology presents. DNA analysis is a powerful and often necessary tool for establishing *the presence or absence* of someone at a crime scene. Readers of this study must remember that this issue cuts both ways.

In the future we must reduce the likelihood of innocent persons being wrongly convicted, just as we must *increase* the chances of guilty parties being identified and held responsible for the crimes they commit. This can be achieved through continued refinement of DNA technology, coupled with better training and procedures to ensure that evidence is skillfully gathered, stored, and submitted for analysis. When used properly and appropriately, DNA analysis can permit us to address the skepticism and doubt that are intrinsic to our system of justice.

Commentary by Peter Neufeld, Esq. and Barry C. Scheck Mr. Scheck Is Professor of Law and Director of Clinical Education Benjamin N. Cardozo School of Law New York, New York

Postconviction DNA exonerations provide a remarkable opportunity to reexamine, with greater insight than ever before, the strengths and weaknesses of our criminal justice system and how they bear on the all-important question of factual innocence. The dimensions of the factual innocence problem exceed the impressive number of postconviction DNA exonerations listed in this report. Indeed, there is a strong scientific basis for believing these matters represent just the tip of a very deep and disturbing iceberg of cases. Powerful proof for this proposition lies with an extraordinary set of data collected by the Federal Bureau of Investigation (FBI) since it began forensic DNA testing in 1989.

Every year since 1989, in about 25 percent of the sexual assault cases referred to the FBI where results could be obtained (primarily by State and local law enforcement), the primary suspect has been excluded by forensic DNA testing. Specifically, FBI officials report that out of roughly 10,000 sexual assault cases since 1989, about 2,000 tests have been inconclusive (usually insufficient high molecular weight DNA to do testing), about 2,000 tests have excluded the primary suspect, and about 6,000 have "matched" or included the primary suspect.[17] The fact that these percentages have remained constant for 7 years, and that the National Institute of Justice's informal survey of private laboratories reveals a strikingly similar 26-percent exclusion rate, strongly suggests that postarrest and postconviction DNA exonerations are tied to some strong, underlying systemic problems that generate erroneous accusations and convictions.

It must be stressed that the sexual assault referrals made to the FBI ordinarily involve cases where (1) identity is at issue (there is no consent defense), (2) the non-DNA evidence linking the suspect to the crime is eyewitness identification, (3) the suspects have been arrested or indicted based on non-DNA evidence, and (4) the biological evidence (sperm) has been recovered from a place (vaginal/rectal/oral swabs or underwear) that makes DNA results on the issue of identity virtually dispositive.

It is, of course, possible that some of the FBI's sexual assault exclusions have included false negatives. False negatives could occur, for example, because of (1) laboratory error; (2) situations where the victim of the assault conceals the existence of a consensual sexual partner within 48 hours of the incident *and* the accused suspect did not ejaculate (if the suspect ejaculated, the DNA should be identified along with the undisclosed sexual partner); or (3) multiple assailant sexual assault cases where none of the apprehended suspects ejaculated (the FBI counts the exclusion of all multiple suspects in a case as just one exclusion). Nonetheless, even with these caveats, it is still

[17] Although there is no sure way to determine what the results would have been on the inconclusive tests if results had been obtainable, it seems a fair assumption, given the strong trends over a 7-year period, that the percentages of exclusions and inclusions of the primary suspect would have run about the same as the cases where results were obtainable. Indeed, since most of the FBI's cases since 1989 involved RFLP tests, which require greater amounts of sample than PCR-based testing, it would be interesting to test this hypothesis by performing PCR tests on some of the old inconclusive cases where primary suspects were either acquitted or convicted.

plain that forensic DNA testing is prospectively exonerating a substantial number of innocent individuals who would have otherwise stood trial, frequently facing the difficult task of refuting mistaken eyewitness identification by a truthful crime victim who would rightly deserve juror sympathy.

Without DNA testing, the prospects of wrongful convictions in these exclusion cases are evident. Even if one assumes half the normal conviction rate (State conviction rates for felony sexual assaults average about 62 percent), one would expect that hundreds of people who have been exonerated by FBI DNA testing in sexual assault cases over the last 7 years would have otherwise been convicted.

The Institute for Law and Justice report does not purport to be more than a quick survey, based primarily on press clippings and summary interviews, of postconviction DNA exoneration cases, and it does not undertake any systematic analysis of them. Since we have been, through the Innocence Project at Cardozo Law School, either attorneys of record or assisting counsel in the vast majority of these cases, we have attempted to investigate, with care and in detail, some of the factors that have led to the conviction of the innocent.[18]

Interestingly, in many respects the reasons for the conviction of the innocent in the DNA cases do not seem strikingly different than those cited by Yale Professor Edwin Borchard in his seminal work, *Convicting the Innocent* (Garden City Pub., 1932), which reviewed 65 cases, and more recently by Hugo Bedau and Michael Radelet in *In Spite of Innocence* (Northeastern University Press, 1992), which reviewed 416 erroneous convictions in death cases from 1900 to 1991. Mistaken eyewitness identification, coerced confessions, unreliable forensic laboratory work, law enforcement misconduct,

[18] While we would be the last to discount the possibility of laboratory error in any DNA testing case, be it an exclusion or an inclusion, great pains have been taken in the postconviction DNA exoneration cases to minimize this factor. First, it must be stressed that these cases, even if involving a homicide, have invariably involved analysis of sperm from swabs (vaginal, oral, or anal) or from clothes worn by the victim. Thus, the chance of inadvertently cross-contaminating the samples with someone else's sperm is remote. Secondly, sexual assault evidence provides an intrinsic redundancy, or internal control, in that the DNA profile from epithelial cells found in samples can be cross-checked against the known DNA profile of the victim. Finally, before convicted prisoners have been released, either through postconviction court orders or clemency grants from governors, the prosecution has insisted upon independent testing of samples by their own experts and elimination samples from other possible sperm donors (husbands or boyfriends) even if it was the prosecution's position at trial that the sperm came from the perpetrator.

and ineffective representation of counsel, singly and often in combination, remain the leading causes of wrongful convictions.

There are, however, historically unique aspects to the DNA exoneration cases. Most significantly, both the postconviction cases described in this report and the prospective sexual assault exclusions produced by the FBI and other laboratories create an opportunity for groundbreaking criminal justice research.

Take, for instance, just the FBI's sexual assault cases. One can confirm among these cases, with greater scientific assurance than is ordinarily provided by a trial verdict, which suspects charged were truly innocent and which suspects were truly guilty. We believe it crucial to identify, prior to any DNA testing, precisely what factors in the investigatory and charging process produced incorrect results in some of these cases and correct results in others. Are there systemic weaknesses that can be identified in eyewitness identification procedures, crime scene investigations, non-DNA laboratory tests (hair, fiber, etc.), police interrogation techniques, or other investigatory methods used by police and prosecutors that are conducive to false or true arrests and convictions? Perhaps there has never been a richer or more exciting set of cases for criminal justice researchers to explore in terms of shedding light on how law enforcement methods impact the crucial problem of factual innocence.

Finally, notwithstanding the research opportunities presented by the postarrest and postconviction DNA exoneration cases as to *how* wrongful accusations and convictions occur, the most significant implication of these cases is already apparent—the extent of factually incorrect convictions in our system must be much greater than anyone wants to believe. Postarrest and postconviction DNA exonerations have invariably involved analysis of sexual assault evidence (sperm), even if a murder charge was involved, that proved the existence of mistaken eyewitness identification. Since there does not seem to be anything inherent in sexual assault cases that would make eyewitnesses more prone to mistakes than in robberies or other serious crimes where the crucial proof is eyewitness identification, it naturally follows that the rate of mistaken identifications and convictions is similar to DNA exoneration cases.

The recently passed anti-terrorism bill contains a sweeping and unprecedented curtailment of the right to obtain postconviction habeas corpus relief in the Federal courts: Strict time limits (1 year in nondeath cases, 3 months in death cases) have been set for filing the writ; State court factual findings are "presumed to be correct"; State court misinterpretations of the United States Constitution are not a basis for relief unless those misinterpretations are "unreasonable"; and all petitioners must show, prior to obtaining a hearing, facts sufficient to establish by clear and convincing evidence that but for the constitutional error, no reasonable factfinder would have found the petitioner guilty. In short, just as DNA testing, the most important technological breakthrough of twentieth century forensic science, demonstrates that the problem of wrongful convictions in America is systemic and serious, Congress and the President, in our view, have eviscerated the "great writ" that for two centuries provided relief to those who were unjustly convicted. Hopefully, before this century closes, as the ramifications of the DNA exoneration cases become better understood, this triumph of political expediency over America's traditional concerns for liberty and justice will be redressed.

SECTION I. INTRODUCTION

> "I had," said he, "come to an entirely erroneous conclusion which shows, my dear Watson, how dangerous it always is to reason from insufficient data."
>
> Arthur Conan Doyle, The Adventure of the Speckled Band

One way to view science is that it is a search for truth.[1] Forensic science is no exception. As Attorney General Janet Reno emphasized, "The use of forensic science as a tool in the search for truth allows justice to be done not only by apprehending the guilty but also by freeing the innocent."[2]

This report describes a study that focused on the freeing of the innocent—persons initially convicted and imprisoned but later released through postconviction forensic use of DNA technology.

Purpose and Scope of the Study

The principal purpose of the study, initiated in June 1995, was to identify and review cases in which convicted persons were released from prison as a result of posttrial DNA testing of evidence. As of early 1996, researchers had found 28 such cases: DNA test results obtained subsequent to trial proved that, on the basis of DNA evidence, the convicted persons could not have committed the crimes for which they were incarcerated.

The study also involved a survey of 40 laboratories that conduct DNA testing.

This report does not probe the strengths or weaknesses of forensic DNA technology when applied to criminal cases.[3] The discussion of DNA instead is limited to its use in exculpating convicted defendants serving prison sentences.

The authors do not claim to be scientific experts in DNA technology. This report cites reference materials that probe technological details more deeply than occurs on these pages.

The balance of this Section outlines the study's design and provides basic background information on forensic DNA identification testing. Sections II and III, respectively, present the study's findings and their policy implications. The final Section consists of brief profiles of the 28 exculpatory cases. A glossary defines DNA-related terms, and the appendix reports DNA test results for some of the exculpated persons profiled in this report.

Study Design

To identify cases that met study criteria—defendant conviction, imprisonment, and subsequent exoneration and release resulting from posttrial exculpatory DNA tests—researchers examined legal and newspaper data bases and interviewed a variety of legal and DNA experts. Once initially identified as likely candidates for the study, cases were verified and assessed through interviews with the involved defense counsel, prosecutors, and forensic laboratory staff; through reviews of court opinions; and, in some instances, through examinations of case files.

For example, initial identification of the Glen Woodall case resulted from an automated search of newspaper data bases, which identified articles about the case in several West Virginia newspapers, the *Philadelphia Inquirer*, and the *Cleveland Plain Dealer*. An opinion by the West Virginia Supreme Court of Appeals in the appeal of Woodall's conviction (*State* v. *Woodall*, 385 S.E.2d 253, W. Va. 1989) contained the name of Woodall's defense attorney, who was called and interviewed at length and who provided materials related to the criminal case.

Those materials described improper activities by Fred Zain, once a serologist for the West Virginia State Police. A phone conversation with the West Virginia assistant attorney general handling the Zain misconduct cases resulted in the receipt of public case documents containing extensive details on Zain's activities related to the Woodall investigation and prosecution.

A review of transcripts from the criminal and, later, civil cases yielded the name of the laboratory that conducted the DNA testing that exculpated Woodall. A lengthy interview was conducted with the laboratory's forensic scientist who performed the DNA tests on the Woodall evidence. He provided documentation related to his examinations in the case.

Cases related to a special West Virginia Supreme Court of Appeals investigation into government misconduct surrounding Woodall's case (438 S.E.2d 501, W. Va. 1993; 445 S.E.2d 165, W. Va. 1994) also were reviewed.

Researchers collected information for the survey of DNA-testing laboratories through telephone interviews. An experienced crime laboratory director assisted the Institute for Law and Justice in conducting the survey.

This study, conducted in a short time period with limited funding, reflects a modest level of analysis and focuses on a relatively small number of cases.

One can state with confidence, however, that as of the study's completion, the 28 cases identified represent most of the situations in the country where convicted felons had been released from prison on the basis of postconviction DNA testing.[4]

Background on Forensic Use of DNA Identification Testing

Perhaps the most significant advance in criminal investigation since the advent of fingerprint identification is the use of DNA technology to help convict criminals or eliminate persons as suspects. DNA analyses on saliva, skin tissue, blood, hair, and semen can now be reliably used to link criminals to crimes. Increasingly accepted during the past 10 years, DNA technology is now widely used by police, prosecutors, defense counsel, and courts in the United States.

An authoritative study on the forensic uses of DNA, conducted by the National Research Council of the National Academy of Sciences, has noted that:

> ...the reliability of DNA evidence will permit it to exonerate some people who would have been wrongfully accused or convicted without it. Therefore, DNA identification is not only a way of securing convictions; it is also a way of excluding suspects who might otherwise be falsely charged with and convicted of serious crimes.[5]

Forensic use of DNA technology in criminal cases began in 1987 when police asked Dr. Alec J. Jeffreys (who coined the term "DNA fingerprints"[6]) of Leicester University (England) to verify a suspect's confession that he was responsible for two rape-murders in the English Midlands.[7] Tests proved that the suspect had not committed the crimes. Police then began obtaining blood samples from several thousand male inhabitants in the area to identify a new suspect.[8] In another 1987 case in England, Robert Melias became the first person convicted of a crime (rape) on the basis of DNA evidence.[9]

In one of the first uses of DNA in a criminal case in the United States, in November 1987, the Circuit Court in Orange County, Florida, convicted Tommy Lee Andrews of rape after DNA tests matched his DNA from a blood sample with that of semen traces found in a rape victim.[10]

Two other important early cases involving DNA testing are *State* v. *Woodall*[11] and *Spencer* v. *Commonwealth.*[12] In *Woodall*, the West Virginia Supreme Court was the first State high court to rule on the admissibility of DNA evidence. The court accepted DNA testing by the defendant, but inconclusive results failed to exculpate Woodall. The court upheld the defendant's conviction for rape, kidnaping, and robbery of two women. Subsequent DNA testing determined that Woodall was innocent, and he was released from prison (see the case profile in Section IV for more details).

The multiple murder trials in Virginia of Timothy Wilson Spencer were the first cases in the United States where the admission of DNA evidence led to guilty verdicts resulting in a death penalty. The Virginia Supreme Court upheld the murder and rape convictions of Spencer, who had been convicted on the basis of DNA testing that matched his DNA with that of semen found in several victims. In *Spencer*, the defendant's attack upon the introduction of DNA evidence was limited to the contention that its novelty should lead the court to "hold off until another day any decision ..."[13] There was no testimony from expert witnesses that challenged the general acceptance of DNA testing among the scientific community.[14]

The first case that seriously challenged a DNA profile's admissibility was *People* v. *Castro*;[15] the New York Supreme Court, in a 12-week pretrial hearing, exhaustively examined numerous issues relating to the admissibility of DNA evidence. Jose Castro was accused of murdering his neighbor and her 2-year-old daughter. A bloodstain on Castro's watch was analyzed for a match to the victim. The court held the following:

- DNA identification theory and practice are generally accepted among the scientific community.
- DNA forensic identification techniques are generally accepted by the scientific community.

- Pretrial hearings are required to determine whether the testing laboratory's methodology was substantially in accord with scientific standards and produced reliable results for jury consideration.

The *Castro* ruling supports the proposition that DNA identification evidence of *exclusion* is more presumptively admissible than DNA identification evidence of *inclusion*. In *Castro*, the court ruled that DNA tests could be used to show that blood on Castro's watch was not his, but tests could not be used to show that the blood was that of his victims.

In *Castro*, the court also recommended extensive discovery requirements for future proceedings, including copies of all laboratory results and reports; explanation of statistical probability calculations; explanations for any observed defects or laboratory errors, including observed contaminants; and chain of custody of documents. These recommendations soon were expanded upon by the Minnesota Supreme Court, in *Schwartz* v. *State*,[16] which noted, "...ideally, a defendant should be provided with the actual DNA sample(s) in order to reproduce the results. As a practical matter, this may not be possible because forensic samples are often so small that the entire sample is used in testing. Consequently, access to the data, methodology, and actual results is crucial...for an independent expert review."[17]

In *Schwartz*, the Supreme Court of Minnesota refused to admit the DNA evidence analyzed by a private forensic laboratory; the court noted the laboratory did not comply with appropriate standards and controls. In particular, the court was troubled by failure of the laboratory to reveal its underlying population data and testing methods. Such secrecy precluded replication of the test.

In summary, courts have successfully challenged improper application of DNA scientific techniques to particular cases, especially when used to declare "matches" based on frequency estimates. However, DNA testing properly applied is generally accepted as admissible under *Frye*[18] or *Daubert*[19] standards.[20] As stated in the National Research Council's 1996 report on DNA evidence, "The state of the profiling technology and the methods for estimating frequencies and related statistics have progressed to the point where the admissibility of properly collected and analyzed DNA data should not be in doubt."[21] At this time, 46 States admit DNA evidence in criminal proceedings. In 43 States, courts have ruled on the technology, and in 3 States, statutes require admission (see exhibit 1).

Exhibit 1. DNA Evidence Admission in Criminal Trials by State

State	DNA Admitted	State	DNA Admitted
Alabama	Yes	Montana	Yes
Alaska	Yes	Nebraska	Yes
Arizona	Yes	Nevada	Statute
Arkansas	Yes	New Hampshire	Yes
California	Yes*	New Jersey	Yes*
Colorado	Yes	New Mexico	Yes
Connecticut	Yes	New York	Yes
Delaware	Yes	North Carolina	Yes
Florida	Yes	North Dakota	No
Georgia	Yes	Ohio	Yes
Hawaii	Yes	Oklahoma	Statute
Idaho	Yes	Oregon	Yes
Illinois	Yes*	Pennsylvania	Yes
Indiana	Yes	Rhode Island	No
Iowa	Yes	South Carolina	Yes
Kansas	Yes	South Dakota	Yes
Kentucky	Yes	Tennessee	Statute
Louisiana	Yes	Texas	Yes
Maine	No	Utah	No
Maryland	Yes*	Vermont	Yes
Massachusetts	Yes	Virginia	Yes
Michigan	Yes	Washington	Yes
Minnesota	Yes	West Virginia	Yes
Mississippi	Yes	Wisconsin	Yes
Missouri	Yes	Wyoming	Yes

* Decision by Intermediate Court of Appeals.

SECTION II. STUDY FINDINGS

Findings pertaining to characteristics of the 28 DNA exculpatory cases identified during the study are discussed first. The Section concludes with the results of the telephone survey of DNA laboratories.

General Characteristics Shared by Many Study Cases

The 28 cases in this study were tried in 14 States and the District of Columbia. The States are Illinois (5 cases), New York (4 cases), Virginia (3 cases), West Virginia (3 cases), Pennsylvania (2 cases), California (2 cases), Maryland, North Carolina, Connecticut, Kansas, Ohio, Indiana, New Jersey, and Texas. Many cases share a number of descriptive characteristics, as noted below.

Most Cases Mid- to Late 1980s

Most cases involved convictions that occurred in the 1980s, primarily mid- to late 1980s, a period when forensic DNA technology was not readily accessible. The earliest case involved a conviction in 1979, the most recent in 1991.

In each of the 28 cases, a defendant was convicted of a crime or crimes and serving a sentence of incarceration. While in prison, each defendant obtained, through an attorney, case evidence for DNA testing and consented to a comparison of the evidence-derived DNA to his own DNA sample. (In *Nelson*, the prosecutor conducted the tests.) In each case, the results showed that there was not a match, and the defendant was ultimately set free. Exhibit 2 presents an overview of the study cases.

Sexual Assault the Most Frequent Crime

All 28 cases involved some form of sexual assault. In six (*Bloodsworth*, *Cruz*, *Hernandez*, *Linscott*, *Nelson*, and *Vasquez*), assailants also murdered their victims. All alleged assailants were male. All victims were female: most were adults, others teenagers or children. All but one case involved a jury trial. (The nonjury case, *Vasquez*, involved a guilty plea from a defendant who had mental disabilities.) Of the cases where the time required for jury deliberations was known, most had verdicts returned in less than 1 day, except for *Kotler*, which required 2 days.

Prison Time Served

The 28 defendants served a total of 197 years in prison (an average of almost 7 years each) before being released as a result of DNA testing. The longest time served was 11 years, the shortest 9 months. For a variety of legal reasons, defendants in several cases continued to remain in prison for months after exculpatory DNA test results. In *Green*, DNA testing was performed after conviction but prior to sentencing.

Exhibit 2. Overview of DNA Study Cases

Case Name/Location	Primary Charges	Date Convicted	Sentence/Served
Alejandro, Gilbert Uvalde, TX	Sexual assault	October 1990	12 yrs/4 yrs
Bloodsworth, Kirk Baltimore, MD	Murder, rape	March 1985	Death, later reduced to life/Almost 9 yrs
Bravo, Mark Diaz Los Angeles Co., CA	Rape	December 1990	8 yrs/3 yrs
Brison, Dale Chester County, PA	Rape, kidnaping	June 1991	18–42 yrs/31/2 yrs
Bullock, Ronnie Chicago, IL	Aggravated sexual assault	May 1984	60 yrs/101/2 yrs
Callace, Leonard White Plains, NY	Sodomy, sexual abuse	March 1987	25–50 yrs/Almost 6 yrs
Chalmers, Terry Leon White Plains, NY	Rape, sodomy	June 1987	12–24 yrs/8 yrs
Cotton, Ronald Burlington, NC	Rape (2 counts)	January 1985 November 1987 (second trial)	Life+54 yrs/101/2 yrs
Cruz, Rolando Chicago, IL	Murder, kidnaping, rape	March 1985	Death/11 yrs
Dabbs, Charles Westchester Co., NY	Rape	April 1984	121/2–20 yrs/7 yrs
Davis, Gerald Wayne Kanawha Co., WV	Kidnaping, sexual assault (2 counts)	May 1986	14–35 yrs/8 yrs
Daye, Frederick Rene San Diego, CA	Rape (2 counts), kidnaping	August 1984	Life/10 yrs
Dotson, Gary Chicago, IL	Rape, aggravated kidnaping	July 1979	25–50 yrs/8 yrs
Green, Edward Washington, DC	Rape	July 1989	Never sentenced/9 months
Hammond, Ricky Hartford, CT	Sexual assault, kidnaping	March 1990	25 yrs and 3 yrs probation/2 yrs
Harris, William O'Dell Charleston, WV	Sexual assault	October 1987	10–20 yrs/7 yrs, then 1 yr home confinement

Exhibit 2. (Continued)

Case Name/Location	Primary Charges	Date Convicted	Sentence/Served
Hernandez, Alejandro Chicago, IL	Murder, kidnaping, rape	March 1985	Death/11 yrs
Honaker, Edward Nelson County, VA	Rape, sexual assault, sodomy	June 1985	3 life terms+34 yrs/10 yrs
Jones, Joe C. Topeka, KS	Rape, aggravated kidnaping	February 1986	Life+10–25 yrs/61/2 yrs
Kotler, Kerry Suffolk County, NY	Rape (2 counts)	February 1982	25–50 yrs/11 yrs
Linscott, Steven Cook County, IL	Murder, rape	November 1982	40 yrs/3 yrs in prison; 7 yrs out on bond
Nelson, Bruce Allegheny Co., PA	Murder, rape	September 1982	Life/9 yrs
Piszczek, Brian Cuyahoga Co., OH	Rape	June 1991	15–25 yrs/4+ yrs
Scruggs, Dwayne Indianapolis, IN	Rape	May 1986	40 yrs/Over 71/2 yrs
Shephard, David Union County, NJ	Rape	September 1984	30 yrs/Almost 10 yrs
Snyder, Walter (Tony) Alexandria, VA	Rape, sodomy	June 1986	45 yrs/Almost 7 yrs
Vasquez, David Arlington Co., VA	Murder, rape	February 1985	35 yrs/5 yrs
Woodall, Glen Huntington, WV	Sexual assault, kidnaping	July 1987	2 life terms+203–335 yrs/4 yrs, then 1 yr under electronic home confinement

Many defendants also qualified for public defenders or appointed counsel. Most defendants appealed their convictions at least once; many appealed several times. Most appeals focused on trial error (e.g., ineffective assistance of counsel) or new evidence. For example, in some cases, the victims recanted their defendant identification testimony.

Prior Police Knowledge of the Defendants

Police knew 15 defendants prior to their arrests, generally through criminal records. It is not known whether, in some cases, that may have influenced police to place suspects in photo spreads and lineups shown to victims and other eyewitnesses.

Evidence Presented during/after Trial: Common Attributes

The 28 cases shared several common themes in the evidence presented during and after trial.

Eyewitness Identification

All cases, except for homicides, involved victim identification both prior to and at trial. Many cases also had additional eyewitness identification, either placing the defendant with the victim or near the crime scene (e.g., in *Bloodsworth*, five witnesses testified that they had seen the defendant with the 9-year-old victim on the day of the murder). Exhibit 3 presents an overview of the evidence and DNA testing in the study cases.

Many defendants presented an alibi defense, frequently corroborated by family or friends. For example, Edward Honaker's alibi was corroborated by his brother, sister-in-law, mother's housemate, and trailer park owner. The alibis apparently were not of sufficient weight to the juries to counter the strength of the eyewitness testimony.

Use of Forensic Evidence

A majority of the cases involved non-DNA-tested forensic evidence that was introduced at trial. Although not pinpointing the defendants, that evidence substantially narrowed the field of possibilities to include them. Typically, those cases involved comparisons of nonvictim specimens of blood, semen, or hair at the crime scene to that of the defendants. Testimony of prosecution experts also was used to explain the reliability and scientific strength of non-DNA evidence to the jury.

Alleged Government Malfeasance or Misconduct

Eight cases, as reported by defense attorneys and reflected in some judges' opinions, involved allegations of government misconduct, including perjured testimony at trial, police and prosecutors who intentionally kept exculpatory evidence from the defense, and intentionally erroneous laboratory tests and expert testimony admitted at trial as evidence. For example:

- In *Honaker*, the defendant's attorney alleged that the government intentionally kept exculpatory evidence from the defense, including information that two of the government's witnesses were secretly hypnotized to enhance their testimony and that the prosecution's criminalist was never told that Honaker had a vasectomy (and could not have been the source of the sperm in the victim).
- In *Cruz*, a supervising officer in the sheriff's department admitted, during the third trial, that he had lied about corroborating the testimony of his deputies in the earlier trials. This testimony focused on Cruz's "dream visions" of the murder.
- In *Kotler*, the government's serologist reportedly lied about his qualifications. In addition, Kotler's attorneys alleged that the government intentionally withheld exculpatory evidence from the defense. For example, police reports stated that the victim did not actually positively identify the defendant's picture but described him only as a "look alike." Furthermore, as recorded in police reports, the victim's description of the defendant was inaccurate for age, height, and weight. The defense was never informed about those reports.
- In cases involving defendants Glen Woodall, William O'Dell Harris, and Gerald Wayne Davis (and his father), the perjured testimony of Fred Zain, a serologist then with the West Virginia State Police, was in large part responsible for the wrongful convictions that ensued. The West Virginia Supreme Court of Appeals, in a special report on Zain's misconduct in more than 130 criminal cases, stated that such behavior included "...overstating the strength of results; ...reporting inconclusive results as conclusive; ...repeatedly altering laboratory records; ...."[1] The report also noted that Zain's irregularities were "the result of systematic practice rather than an occasional inadvertent error." In addition, the report stated that Zain's "supervisors may have ignored or concealed complaints of his misconduct."[2]
- In *Alejandro*, the defendant was also wrongfully convicted by expert testimony from Fred Zain, who had moved from West Virginia to Texas and worked for the Bexar County crime laboratory. In July 1994, a Uvalde County grand jury indicted Zain for perjury, tampering with government records, and fabricating evidence. As of early 1996, charges of tampering and of fabricating evidence had been

dropped, leaving three charges for aggravated perjury in effect, for which Zain reportedly seeks dismissal on statute of limitations grounds.

Exhibit 3. Overview of Selected Evidence and DNA Testing

Defendant	Selected Evidence	DNA Testing
Alejandro, Gilbert	DNA evidence testimony; victim ID	Restriction Fragment Length Polymorphism (RFLP) tests of semen stain on victim's nightgown excluded Alejandro.
Bloodsworth, Kirk	Five witness IDs; self-incriminating statements	Polymerase Chain Reaction (PCR) test of panties excluded Bloodsworth.
Bravo, Mark Diaz	Victim ID; blood analysis; misrepresentation	RFLP test of blanket, sheet, and victim's panties excluded Bravo.
Brison, Dale	Victim ID; hair analysis; weak alibi	RFLP test of semen-stained panties excluded Brison.
Bullock, Ronnie	Two victim IDs; police ID; proximity of residence	PCR test of semen-stained panties excluded Bullock. DNA tests on vaginal and anal swabs were inconclusive.
Callace, Leonard	Victim ID; blood analysis; weak alibi	RFLP test of semen-stained jeans excluded Callace.
Chalmers, Terry Leon	Victim ID; weak alibi	PCR test of two vaginal swabs excluded Chalmers.
Cotton, Ronald	Victim ID; similarity of shoes and flashlight	PCR test of vaginal swab and underwear excluded Cotton.
Cruz, Rolando	Alleged "dream visions" of the murder; inculpatory witness statements	PCR test of semen-stained underwear excluded Cruz and included Brian Dugan.
Dabbs, Charles	Victim ID; blood analysis	RFLP test of semen-stained panties excluded Dabbs.
Davis, Gerald Wayne	Victim ID; semen analysis	PCR test of the victim's underwear excluded Davis. No DNA found matching the victim from DNA tests done on Davis' bedsheets and underwear.
Daye, Frederick Rene	Victim ID; witness ID; blood analysis; misrepresentation	PCR test of semen-stained jeans excluded Daye.
Dotson, Gary	Victim ID; semen analysis; hair analysis	RFLP test of panties was inconclusive. PCR test of panties excluded Dotson and included victim's boyfriend.

Exhibit 3. (Continued)

Defendant	Selected Evidence	DNA Testing
Green, Edward	Victim ID; blood analysis	RFLP test of the victim's clothing excluded Green.
Hammond, Ricky	Victim ID; victim ID of car; hair analysis; weak alibi	RFLP and blood tests excluded Hammond.
Harris, William O'Dell	Victim ID; semen analysis	PCR test of evidence slide excluded Harris.
Hernandez, Alejandro	Self-incriminating and inculpatory statements; inculpatory witness statements	PCR test of semen-stained underwear excluded Hernandez and included Brian Dugan.
Honaker, Edward	Victim ID; witness ID; hair analysis; similarity of clothing	PCR test of vaginal swab excluded Honaker and both of victim's boyfriends.
Jones, Joe C.	Victim ID; proximity to crime scene; similarity of pants; 2 witness IDs	PCR test of partial vaginal swab excluded Jones.
Kotler, Kerry	Victim ID; non-DNA genetic analysis	PCR test of panties excluded Kotler and victim's husband.
Linscott, Steven	Blood analysis; hair analysis; "dream confession"	Pretrial DNA tests were inconclusive. PCR test excluded Linscott.
Nelson, Bruce	Testimony of codefendant, self-incriminating statement	RFLP test excluded Nelson.
Piszczek, Brian	Victim ID; weak alibi	PCR test of vaginal and anal swabs and nightgown excluded Piszczek.
Scruggs, Dwayne	Victim ID; similarity of boots	PCR test of vaginal swab and bloodstain excluded Scruggs.
Shephard, David	Victim ID; blood analysis; weak alibi	DNA test of panty liner excluded Shephard.
Snyder, Walter (Tony)	Victim ID; similarity of clothing; blood analysis; weak alibi	PCR test of vaginal swab excluded Snyder.
Vasquez, David	Witness ID; no alibi; confession; hair analysis	PCR test of evidence matched Timothy Spencer. Attempts to compare hair with blood samples were inconclusive.
Woodall, Glen	Blood analysis; hair analysis; victim ID; similarity of clothing	PCR and RFLP tests of vaginal swabs and clothing excluded Woodall.

Evidence Discovered after Trial

In most of the cases in this study, DNA test results represented newly discovered evidence obtained after completion of the trials. States have time limits on filing motions for new trials on the basis of newly discovered evidence. For example, in Virginia, new evidence must be presented by motion within 21 days after the trial.[3] Thus, the *Honaker*, *Snyder*, and *Vasquez* cases required a pardon from Virginia's governor to release the defendants from prison.

In some of the study cases, prosecutors waived time limits when presented with the DNA exculpatory results. However, prosecutors also have contested defendants' attempts to release evidence for DNA testing.

States also differ in the legislation and procedures pertaining to postconviction appointment of counsel and to authorization to pay for the DNA testing. Many cases involved indigents.

DNA Testing

The DNA testing phase of these cases also has common characteristics. Nearly all the defendants had their tests performed by private laboratories. The tests were conducted using blood from defendants, blood or blood-related evidence from victims, and semen stains on articles of the victims' clothing or on nearby items (a blanket was tested in one case). In over half the cases, the prosecution either conducted a DNA test totally independent of that of the defense or sent test results obtained by the defendant's laboratory to a different one to determine whether the laboratory used by the defense interpreted test results properly.

Eight laboratories used Restriction Fragment Length Polymorphism (RFLP) DNA testing, 17 conducted Polymerase Chain Reaction (PCR) testing, and 2 used both tests. For one case, the type of DNA test conducted is unknown.

Preservation of Evidence

In some cases, evidence samples had deteriorated to the point where DNA testing could not be performed. In *Brison*, the laboratory could not test cotton swabs from the rape kit but, instead, tested a semen stain from the victim's underwear. In *Daye*, after the appellate court affirmed the defendant's conviction and the State Supreme Court denied certification, the evidence was about to be destroyed when Daye's attorney filed to stay the destruction in order to conduct DNA testing.

The chain of custody in some of the cases also demonstrated a lack of adherence to proper procedures. Authorities on the subject note that the "mishandling of real evidence affects the integrity of the factfinding process."[4] In *Dabbs*, the defendant's attorneys reported that the defense was initially advised by the prosecution that the evidence (victim's underwear that contained a semen stain) had been destroyed (a conclusion based on failure of authorities to find the evidence in police or court custody). Eventually, the defense found the evidence at the county crime laboratory.

Results of DNA Laboratory Survey

Conducted in June 1995, the nationwide telephone survey of 40 public and private laboratories that performed DNA tests sought answers to such questions as: From the time the laboratories began DNA testing, how many cases have they handled? Of that number, what percentage yielded results that excluded defendants as sources of the DNA evidence or were inconclusive?

The 40 surveyed laboratories yielded 19 whose available data were sufficient for the purposes of this study. The 19 included 13 at the State/local level, 4 in the private sector, an armed forces laboratory, and the FBI's laboratory.

Most of the laboratories had initiated DNA testing only within the previous few years. Twelve began testing between 1990 and 1992. Three of the four private laboratories began in 1986 or 1987, while the FBI started DNA testing in 1988.

Seven of the laboratories reported using RFLP testing; four, PCR testing; and eight, both types of tests.

The 19 laboratories reported that, since they began testing, they had received evidence in 21,621 cases for DNA analysis, with the FBI accounting for 10,060 cases. Three of the 4 private laboratories averaged 2,400 each; the State and local laboratories averaged 331 each.

In about 23 percent of the 21,621 cases, DNA test results excluded suspects, according to respondents. An additional 16 percent of the cases, approximately, yielded inconclusive results, often because the test samples had deteriorated or were too small. Inconclusive results aside, test results in the balance of the cases did not exclude the suspect.

The FBI reported that, in the 10,060 cases it received, DNA testing results were about 20 percent inconclusive and 20 percent exclusion; the other 18 laboratories (11,561 cases) reported about 13 percent and 26 percent, respectively.[19]

Unfortunately, the laboratories were unable to provide more details. They did not maintain data bases that would permit categorization of DNA test results by type of offense and other criteria. What happened to the suspects who were excluded through DNA testing also cannot be determined. Were they released, or were they charged on the basis of other evidence, for example?

Thus, only the most general information is known about the results of DNA testing by laboratories. To obtain more detailed information would require a comprehensive research project.

Section III. Policy Implications

The 28 cases examined by the study raise issues that have policy implications for the criminal justice system. The most significant are presented below.[1]

Reliability of Eyewitness Testimony

In the majority of the cases, given the absence of DNA evidence at the trial, eyewitness testimony was the most compelling evidence. Clearly, however, those eyewitness identifications were wrong. In one of the clearest examples of eyewitness testimony overwhelmingly influencing the jury, the Pennsylvania Intermediate Court of Appeals commented on the evidence in the Dale Brison case:

> The Commonwealth's evidence consisted primarily of the victim's identification testimony. However, the victim's stab wounds in addition to the weather and reduced visibility may well have affected the victim's ability to accurately view her assailant, and thus, she may have been prompted to identify appellant merely because she remembered seeing him in the neighborhood. Moreover, the victim did not specifically describe any of her assailant's facial

[19] If inconclusive cases were omitted, the exclusion rate for the FBI would be approximately 25 percent, and the average exclusion rate for the other 18 laboratories would be about 30 percent.

> characteristics to the police. There was also no conclusive physical evidence, aside from a single hair sample which may have been consistent with any male of [A]frican-[A]merican descent, linking appellant to the crime.[2]

This points conclusively to the need in the legal system for improved criteria for evaluating the reliability of eyewitness identification.

In *Neil* v. *Biggers*,[3] the U.S. Supreme Court established criteria that jurors may use to evaluate the reliability of eyewitness identifications. However, the reliability of eyewitness testimony has been criticized extensively in the literature.[4] In a recent interview, Dr. Elizabeth Loftus, one of the best-known critics of the reliability of eyewitness identification, commented on the role of DNA testing in exonerating innocent persons who served time in prison. Dr. Loftus noted that a significant factor is the potential susceptibility of eyewitnesses to suggestions from police, whether intentional or unintentional. As reported, Dr. Loftus stated that there is "pressure that comes from the police [who] want to see the crime solved, but there is also a psychological pressure that is understandable on the part of the victim who wants to see the bad guy caught and wants to feel that justice is done."[5]

Dr. Loftus has recommended more open-ended questioning of victims by the police to avoid leading questions. In addition, Dr. Loftus and others have recommended use of expert testimony regarding the pros and cons of relying on eyewitness testimony.[6]

Reliability of Non-DNA Analyses of Forensic Evidence Compared to DNA Testing

In many of the study cases, according to documentation examined and those interviewed, scientific experts had convinced juries that non-DNA analyses of blood or hair were reliable enough to clearly implicate the defendants. Scientific conclusions based on non-DNA analyses, however, were proven less discriminating and reliable than those based on DNA tests. These findings point to the need for the scientific community to take into account the reliability of non-DNA forensic analyses vis-à-vis DNA testing in identifying the sources of biological evidence.

In a recent habeas corpus hearing in a murder case, a U.S. district court held that expert testimony on microscopic hair comparisons was inadmissible under the *Daubert* standard.[7] The court cited studies documenting a high error rate and found that there are no accepted probability standards for human hair identification. The court ruled that in this case the expert's hair testimony was "imprecise and speculative, and its probative value was outweighed by its prejudicial effect."[8]

Competence and Reliability of DNA Laboratory Procedures

One of the lasting effects of the O.J. Simpson case will likely be greater scrutiny by defense lawyers of the prosecution's forensic DNA evidence presented in criminal cases. In the Simpson case, the defense, in essence, put the crime laboratory on trial. The National Research Council (NRC) report entitled *DNA Technology in Forensic Science* states:

> There is no substantial dispute about the underlying [DNA] scientific principles. However, the adequacy of laboratory procedures and the competence of the experts who testify should remain open to inquiry.[9]

The NRC report recommends some degree of standardization to ensure quality and reliability. The report recommends that each forensic laboratory engaged in DNA testing must have a formal, detailed program of quality assurance and quality control. The report also states:

> Quality-assurance programs in individual laboratories alone are insufficient to ensure high standards. External mechanisms are needed to ensure adherence to the practices of quality assurance. Potential mechanisms include individual certification, laboratory accreditation, and state or federal regulation.[10]

As recently reported by the American Society of Crime Laboratory Directors, 32 public DNA laboratories have been accredited. In addition, one private laboratory is accredited.[11]

Whether laboratories that conduct DNA tests possess the requisite qualifications has significant cost implications for the criminal justice system in terms of reducing the number of redundant DNA tests. In many cases in this study, both prosecution and defense obtained independent DNA tests of the biological stain evidence. Although independent examinations are common in areas that are more open to interpretation (e.g., mental fitness for trial), DNA testing, for exculpatory purposes, should be performed in a qualified laboratory, and the results, if they exculpate the suspect, should be accepted by both parties. Such acceptance would seem more likely if DNA tests were performed by laboratories that all parties agreed were qualified.

Preservation of Evidence for DNA Testing

In some States, sentenced felons may experience difficulty obtaining access to evidence for DNA testing. With an increasing volume of criminal cases, some police agencies destroy evidence when defendants have exhausted their appeals. Even when defendants obtain access to the evidence, it may be too deteriorated for DNA testing. In some of the study cases, insufficient evidence prevented laboratories from conducting Restriction Fragment Length Polymorphism (RFLP) testing, but Polymerase Chain Reaction (PCR) testing was still possible.

Preserving biological stain evidence and maintaining the proper chain of custody of the evidence are essential for successful DNA testing.[12] At the trial stage, however, the U.S. Supreme Court has ruled that unless a criminal defendant can show bad faith on the part of the police, failure to preserve potentially useful evidence does not constitute a denial of due process of law.[13] After a defendant's conviction, prosecutors are not required by constitutional duty to preserve evidence indefinitely. As noted earlier, in *Daye*, the evidence was about to be destroyed when his attorney filed to stay the destruction to conduct what turned out to be an exculpatory DNA test.

Training in DNA Forensic Uses

The introduction of DNA technology into the criminal trial setting is likely to create uncertainty, spawned in part by the complexity of the technology, and also to possibly generate unrealistic expectations of the technology's power in the minds of some or all of the players: prosecution, defense, judges, and jurors. The scientific complexities of the technology may influence all parties to rely more heavily on expert testimony than on other types of evidence.

As the use of DNA technology becomes more widely publicized, juries will come to expect it, like fingerprint evidence. This will place more pressure on prosecutors to use the technology whenever possible, especially as the cost decreases. Prosecutors must be trained on when to use the technology and how to interpret results for the jury.

When the prosecution uses DNA evidence, the defense will be forced to attack it through expert testimony. The defense must rebut the persuasiveness of the evidence for the jury. As stated in the NRC report, "Mere cross examination by a defense attorney inexperienced in the science of DNA testing will not be sufficient."[14] Thus, defense counsel as well as the prosecution and judiciary must receive training in the forensic uses of DNA technology.

Third-Party Consensual Sex Sources

The primary objective of the defense in using DNA testing in rape cases is to show that the defendant is excluded as the source of the semen evidence. Even when exclusion is established, the prosecution may be motivated, as in *Davis*, to eliminate as suspects any and all consensual sex partners as sources of semen in rape cases. During the first trial of Gerald Wayne Davis, the prosecution contended that the semen in the victim came from Davis. After DNA testing had excluded Davis as the source of the semen, the prosecution contended, in the second trial, that Davis could have still raped the victim but not ejaculated and that the semen in the victim could have come from the victim's fiancé just prior to the rape. The prosecution never obtained a blood sample from the fiancé because he died before the second trial.

A question under the law is whether third parties can be compelled to provide biological evidence for DNA testing. In some cases, the government refused to release defendants after exculpatory DNA results until third parties were located and tested. Kerry Kotler was held for an additional year after his exculpatory DNA test so the government could test the victim's husband. Edward Honaker was held for an additional 9 months after his exculpatory DNA test so the government could test the victim's boyfriend and "secret lover."

Multiple-Defendant Crimes

The DNA technology used to analyze biological evidence from crime scenes must not be oversold as an exculpatory tool—it does have limitations. Multiple-suspect crimes present a particular problem for use of DNA identification as a crime-solving tool. In multiple-suspect sexual assaults without eyewitnesses, such as a rape-murder, it is possible that only one of the suspects ejaculated in, or even raped, the victim. In such cases, DNA testing of semen would seem likely to exculpate one or more of the suspects. This type of situation presents a real dilemma for police and prosecutors. Because of exculpatory DNA tests on semen and possibly other exculpatory evidence (e.g., an alibi, lack of other physical evidence), pressure mounts on prosecutors to release one or more of the suspects. The only other evidence against them may be the testimony of a suspect who is matched to the crime by DNA analysis.

In *Dabbs*, for example, the victim testified that she was dragged into an alley and raped by one man while two other men held her down. The police arrested Dabbs on the basis of identification of him by the victim, a distant cousin. The other alleged assailants were never identified or arrested. The DNA test showed that the semen evidence from the victim did not match Dabbs. One theory of the case, however, was that Dabbs participated in the crime but was not the rapist. The prosecutor ultimately dismissed the original indictment against Dabbs because of the DNA results and the reluctance of the victim to testify at a new trial.

Posttrial Relief

Most States have a time limit on presenting evidence newly discovered after trial, conviction, and sentencing. The reason for limiting the time to file appeals based on new evidence is to ensure the integrity of the trial process and jury verdicts. Many DNA issues in the study cases were not raised until the postconviction stages. Absent constitutional issues, many State procedures, as in Virginia,[15] may preclude consideration of new exculpatory DNA evidence at postconviction stages. Some of the study defendants, after receiving exculpatory DNA results, were released only by agreement of the prosecutor; sometimes they needed a pardon by the governor.

Some States, such as Oregon, permit judges to use discretion to waive new-evidence rules and set aside verdicts or order new trials.[16] Thus, some States may allow an out-of-time motion for a new trial when newly discovered evidence clearly serves the interests of justice.[17]

At postconviction stages, appointment of counsel and payment for DNA testing become issues for indigents. While some appeals courts have ordered State-paid DNA testing for indigents where justified (e.g., where the overall case against the defendant is weak), other court rulings deny such relief, especially where the exculpatory value is speculative.[18] As DNA testing to exculpate convicted persons becomes more widespread, States need to consider these issues.

Future DNA Forensic Uses

The momentum is growing, spurred in part by the public's education from the Simpson trial, for DNA testing in criminal cases. Juries may begin to question cases where the prosecutor does not offer "conclusive" DNA test results if the evidence is available for testing. More defense attorneys in court-appointed cases may file motions for DNA testing and request the State to pay for the tests (this issue may also be raised as a *Brady* motion for the prosecutor to conduct the tests).

The shift will be for more DNA testing in pretrial stages. Prosecutors should find that DNA testing is as helpful to them as to the defense in excluding suspects early in the investigation. This will enable the police and prosecution to save money in the long run by focusing investigations in more fruitful directions.

In Britain, mass DNA screening in search of suspects has, in recent years, produced arrests in several highly publicized cases. The most recent case involved the rape-murder of a 15-year-old South Wales girl.[19] The South Wales constabulary obtained saliva swab samples from over 2,000 men who lived in the vicinity of the murder. Police went door-to-door inviting men to a makeshift laboratory to submit the samples. The saliva samples were used to develop DNA profiles to compare to the DNA profile obtained from the assailant's semen.

British law does not permit compulsory sampling, but the police made it clear that anyone who refused would become the subject of intense police investigation. A 19-year-old resident of the victim's neighborhood was arrested when his saliva sample was the only one of the thousands taken that could not be eliminated.

Such DNA dragnet methods, while employed sparingly in Great Britain, may increase as the ease and affordability of DNA testing improves. It is unlikely that such mass-testing methods would gain favor in the United States. Constitutional protections against self-incrimination and unreasonable searches and seizures, as well as the American public's zealous protection of privacy rights, would preclude such DNA dragnet practices from being implemented in this country.

SECTION IV. PROFILES OF DNA EXCULPATORY CASES

Presented alphabetically, each profile of the 28 DNA exculpatory cases identified by the study consists of a brief summary of the facts of the case, key prosecution evidence admitted during trial, postconviction challenges, DNA testing results, and case conclusion.

Gilbert Alejandro (Uvalde County, Texas)

Factual Background

On the evening of April 27, 1990, a woman in her fifties came home and was attacked from behind by a man. The man placed a pillow over her head and sexually assaulted her. He then fled the house. The woman could not describe the man except for basic physical size. She also noted that the man was wearing some kind of cap, a gray T-shirt, and dark-colored shorts. The police canvassed the area and questioned three men, one of whom was wearing clothes matching the victim's description. The police did not detain them. The victim picked out Alejandro from his photograph in a mug book.

In October 1990 Gilbert Alejandro was convicted of aggravated sexual assault by a Uvalde County jury. He was sentenced to 12 years in prison.

Prosecutor's Evidence at Trial

The prosecution based its case on several points:

- The victim identified Alejandro from a police mug shot.
- The victim identified Alejandro in court (although she stated that she had a pillow over her head during the assault).
- Fred Zain, the chief forensic expert for Bexar County, Texas, testified that a DNA test of Alejandro's sample matched DNA found on the victim's clothing "and could only have originated from him [Alejandro]."
- Alejandro's only alibi was from his mother, who testified that he was at home at the time of the assault.

Postconviction Challenges

Bexar County performed the forensic laboratory work in this case for the Uvalde County prosecutor's office. Bexar County discovered that the State's forensic expert in this case, Fred Zain (see also the Gerald Wayne Davis, William O'Dell Harris, and Glen Woodall cases), had falsified results and lied about his credentials when he was employed as a State police serologist in West Virginia. When Alejandro's lawyers were informed of this, they filed a writ of habeas corpus. At this time, Alejandro was released to his parents and placed on electronic monitoring.

On July 26, 1994, a Uvalde County District Court heard Alejandro's petition. Present at this hearing were an original trial juror, the original jury foreman, and a Bexar County forensic DNA analyst. The two jurors testified that they based their guilty verdict solely on Zain's testimony and without his testimony the jury would have acquitted on the basis of reasonable doubt. The DNA analyst testified that results from at least one other DNA test had excluded Alejandro. He also testified that the test to which Zain testified was inconclusive and could not have been the basis of a conviction.

DNA Results

In July 1990 the original DNA tests done in this case—the ones Zain testified were inculpatory—were inconclusive. A Restriction Fragment Length Polymorphism (RFLP) test performed by the Bexar County crime laboratory on October 3, 1990, excluded Alejandro as the source of the semen left on the victim's nightgown. The district court also reported that an additional test was done on December 19, 1990, after the trial, and it too excluded Alejandro. According to the district court's findings of fact, Fred Zain knew of these exculpatory results and failed to report them to anyone.

Conclusion

As a result of the findings of fact by the district court, the court of criminal appeals overturned Alejandro's conviction and released him to stand trial again without Zain's testimony. The district attorney, however, declined to prosecute the case. On September 21, 1994, Alejandro was released from electronic monitoring and all charges were dismissed. Alejandro served 4 years of his sentence. On June 27, 1995, he was awarded $250,000 in a civil suit against Bexar County.

Kirk Bloodsworth (Baltimore, Maryland)

Factual Background

On July 25, 1984, a 9-year-old girl was found dead in a wooded area. She had been beaten with a rock, sexually assaulted, and strangled.

Kirk Bloodsworth was convicted on March 8, 1985, of sexual assault, rape, and first-degree premeditated murder. A Baltimore County judge sentenced Bloodsworth to death.

Prosecutor's Evidence at Trial

The prosecution based its case on several points:

- An anonymous caller tipped police that Bloodsworth had been seen with the girl earlier in the day.
- A witness identified Bloodsworth from a police sketch compiled by five witnesses.
- The five witnesses testified that they had seen Bloodsworth with the little girl.
- Bloodsworth had told acquaintances he had done something "terrible" that day that would affect his marriage.
- In his first police interrogation, Bloodsworth mentioned a "bloody rock," even though no weapons were known of at the time.
- Testimony was given that a shoe impression found near the victim's body was made by a shoe that matched Bloodsworth's size.

Postconviction Challenges

In 1986 Bloodsworth's attorney filed an appeal contending the following: Bloodsworth mentioned the bloody rock because the police had one on the table next to him while they interrogated him; the terrible thing mentioned to friends was that he had failed to buy his wife a taco salad as he had promised; and police withheld information from defense attorneys relating to the possibility of another suspect.

The Maryland Court of Appeals overturned Bloodsworth's conviction in July 1986 because of the withheld information. He was retried, and a jury convicted him a second time. This time Bloodsworth was sentenced to two consecutive life terms.

After an appeal of the second conviction was denied, Bloodsworth's lawyer moved to have the evidence released for more sophisticated testing than was available at the time of trial. The prosecution agreed, and in April

1992 the victim's panties and shorts, a stick found near the murder scene, reference blood samples from Bloodsworth and the victim, and an autopsy slide were sent to Forensic Science Associates (FSA) for Polymerase Chain Reaction (PCR) testing.

DNA Results

The FSA report, issued on May 17, 1993, stated that semen on the autopsy slide was insufficient for testing. It also stated that a small semen stain had been found on the panties.

The report indicated that the majority of DNA associated with the epithelial fraction had the same genotype as the semen due to the low level of epithelial cells present in the stain. It was an expected result, according to the report. Finally, the report concluded that Bloodsworth's DNA did not match any of the evidence received for testing. FSA did, however, request a fresh sample of Bloodsworth's blood for retesting in accord with questions about proper labeling on the original sample.

On June 3, 1993, FSA issued a second report that stated its findings regarding Bloodsworth's DNA were replicated and that he could not be responsible for the stain on the victim's underwear (see appendix for complete results).

Conclusion

On June 25, 1993, the FBI conducted its own test of the evidence and discovered the same results as FSA. In Maryland, new evidence can be presented no later than 1 year after the final appeal. Prosecutors joined a petition with Bloodsworth's attorneys to grant Bloodsworth a pardon. A Baltimore County circuit judge ordered Bloodsworth released from prison on June 28, 1993. Maryland's governor pardoned Bloodsworth in December 1993. Bloodsworth served almost 9 years of the second sentence, including 2 years on death row.

Mark Diaz Bravo (Los Angeles County, California)

Factual Background

On February 20, 1990, a patient at the psychiatric hospital where Bravo worked claimed she had been raped in an alcove earlier that afternoon. During the course of police interviews, she named several different people as her assailant. One of those she named was Bravo. She later stated she was sure Bravo was the attacker.

A Los Angeles County jury found Mark Diaz Bravo guilty of rape in 1990. He was sentenced by the court to a prison term of 8 years.

Prosecutor's Evidence at Trial

The prosecution based its case on several points:

- The victim named Bravo as the assailant and made an in-court identification.
- Bravo had misrepresented himself in the past on applications and on his business card.
- Blood tests done on a blanket near the crime scene showed a blood type consistent with Bravo's blood type, which is found in only 3 percent of the population.
- Bravo's alibi defense was not aggressively pursued.

Postconviction Challenges

Bravo's appeal to the intermediate court of appeals was denied. Before his appeal was decided in 1992, he filed a postconviction motion in the Superior Court of Los Angeles County. In 1993 a superior court judge granted Bravo's motion to release a blanket, a sheet, and a pair of panties to the defense for DNA testing.

DNA Results

Prosecutors received a report from Cellmark Diagnostics on December 24, 1993, stating that none of the tested semen had DNA that matched Bravo's.

Conclusion

On January 4, 1994, Bravo's lawyer filed a writ of habeas corpus. A Los Angeles County Superior Court judge ordered Bravo to be released on January 6, 1994. The judge stated that Bravo had not received a fair trial, that the victim had recanted her testimony, that Bravo's alibi was unimpeachable, and that the DNA tests were irrefutable. On January 7, 1994, Bravo was released from prison after serving 3 years of his sentence.

Dale Brison (Chester County, Pennsylvania)

Factual Background

On the evening of July 14, 1990, the victim was walking from a convenience store to her home when an assailant came from behind her, put one hand on her throat and one on her waist, and forced her to walk with him. The assailant stabbed her in the side as they walked, and the victim lost consciousness. When she awoke, the assailant was walking her to some bushes near an apartment complex. The assailant then repeatedly assaulted the victim sexually.

In a jury trial before the Chester County Court of Common Pleas, Dale Brison was convicted of rape, kidnaping, aggravated assault, carrying a prohibited offensive weapon, and three counts of involuntary deviate sexual intercourse. Brison was sentenced to 18 to 42 years of imprisonment. His term was 8 to 20 years for rape and 4 to 10 years for assault, to be served consecutively. He also received 6 to 12 years for each of the involuntary deviate sexual intercourse convictions (although each of these was to run concurrently, they were to be served consecutively with the other sentences). Brison sought DNA testing during the trial, but his request was denied.

Prosecutor's Evidence at Trial

The prosecution based its case on several points:

- There were two separate victim identifications of Brison near the victim's apartment building.
- A hair sample from the scene of the crime was consistent with Brison's.
- Brison's alibi, sleeping on the couch of his home, was corroborated only by his mother.

Postconviction Challenges

In 1992 the Pennsylvania Superior Court ruled (618 A.2d 420) that DNA testing must be performed if the evidence had been maintained and the semen stain from the victim's underwear was not badly degraded. It also ruled that the burden of the cost of this test was upon the Commonwealth.

DNA Results

Cellmark Diagnostics reported that no result was discernible from the vaginal swab, but the semen stain from the victim's panties yielded results that exculpated Brison as the assailant.

Conclusion

After the tests were performed, the district attorney's office conducted its own. Results matched those of the first one, and Brison was freed after serving $3^1/_2$ years of his sentence.

Ronnie Bullock (Chicago, Illinois)

Factual Background

On March 18, 1983, a 9-year-old girl was walking to school when a man dressed like a police officer approached her. He then chased the girl, forced her into a car, drove to a nearby alley, and raped her. On April 18, 1983, in the same area, a 12-year-old girl reported that a man displaying a badge chased her, forced her into a car, drove to an alley, and raped her.

Bullock was charged in both incidents, but charges stemming from the second were dropped. Ronnie Bullock was convicted of aggravated criminal sexual assault by a Cook County jury in May 1984. A judge sentenced Bullock to 60 years in prison for deviate sexual assault and 15 concurrent years for aggravated kidnaping.

Prosecutor's Evidence at Trial

The prosecution based its case on several points:

- A police officer identified Bullock from a composite sketch compiled by the two victims.
- Both victims identified Bullock in a police lineup.
- Bullock lived in the area where the rapes occurred.

Postconviction Challenges

Immediately following Bullock's conviction, he insisted that the evidence be impounded. This motion was approved, and the judge ordered that the victim's panties be stored in the circuit court clerk's office freezer. An appeals court upheld Bullock's conviction in March 1987. Bullock also filed a motion for postconviction relief, which was denied in October 1990. He then submitted a motion in 1993 to have the evidence released for DNA tests. The prosecution agreed to this motion; it was granted in June 1993. There was a delay, however, between the granting of the motion and Cellmark Diagnostics' test because some of the evidence (including the victim's panties) had disappeared. Bullock's attorneys eventually found the materials and sent them to Cellmark Diagnostics.

DNA Results

The report from Cellmark Diagnostics, completed in October 1994, stated that PCR testing was performed on a sperm and nonsperm fraction of the victim's panties, a rectal swab, the blood of the victim, and the blood of Bullock. No conclusions could be reached from the rectal swab due to an insufficient quantity of human DNA. The report stated that Bullock was excluded as the source of both the sperm and the nonsperm fractions in the semen stain on the victim's panties (see appendix for complete results).

Conclusion

On October 14, 1994, Bullock was released without bond but ordered to remain confined to his parents' house on electronic monitoring. The prosecution wanted to run its own tests on the panties, so a hearing was scheduled for November 23, 1994. When the Cook County laboratory arrived at the same conclusion, a judge dismissed the charges, and the district attorney's office declined to prosecute in a new trial. Bullock served 10^{1}/2 years of his sentence.

Leonard Callace (White Plains, New York)

Factual Background

In January 1985 a teenage girl was walking to her car in the parking lot of a shopping center. She was accosted by two men at knife point and forced into a nearby car. One man, allegedly Callace, sexually assaulted the victim repeatedly while the other man watched from the front seat. The second man was never identified.

A Suffolk County jury took 1 hour to convict Leonard Callace of sodomy (four counts), sexual abuse (three counts), wrongful imprisonment, and criminal possession of a weapon. Callace rejected a plea bargain that would have given him 4 months in prison if he pled to a lesser charge. On March 24, 1987, Callace was sentenced to 25 to 50 years in prison.

Prosecutor's Evidence at Trial

The prosecution based its case on several points:

- A sketch by police artists resembled Callace.
- The victim identified Callace from a photo array and made an in-court identification.
- The blood group of the semen was type A, the same as Callace's.
- Callace's alibi was uncorroborated.

Postconviction Challenges

Callace's conviction was affirmed on appeal and leave to appeal to the court of appeals was denied. While in prison, Callace learned about DNA testing and how it was used to free a former inmate (see case summary of Charles Dabbs). He asked his attorney about the original trial evidence.

Callace's attorney remembered two things from the original trial record. First, the victim had just picked up her jeans from the cleaners. Second, the victim spit out semen onto the jeans after one of the assaults. Therefore, any semen on those jeans would have come from the assailant; if it did not match Callace's, he could be freed. The defense used this information to secure the jeans from the prosecution for DNA testing at Lifecodes, Inc. On June 27, 1991, a Suffolk County Court judge granted Callace's motion to consider DNA tests as "new evidence" (573 N.Y.S.2d 137). The judge also ruled that if the samples did not match, he would hold a hearing to consider postconviction relief for Callace.

DNA Results

The RFLP analysis performed by Lifecodes, Inc., on the victim's jeans showed that DNA in the semen stains did not match Callace's.

Conclusion

On October 5, 1992, Callace was released from prison. The prosecution dismissed all charges against Callace and declined to prosecute in a new trial because of the DNA evidence and the reluctance of the victim to endure another trial. Callace served almost 6 years of his sentence.

Terry Leon Chalmers (White Plains, New York)

Factual Background

On August 18, 1986, a woman was raped, and Terry Chalmers was arrested for the crime.

He was convicted by a Westchester County jury on June 9, 1987, of rape, sodomy, robbery, and two counts of grand larceny. The court sentenced Chalmers to 12 to 24 years in prison.

Prosecutor's Evidence at Trial

The prosecution based its case against Chalmers on several points:

- The victim identified Chalmers from a police photo array.
- The victim identified Chalmers in two separate police lineups and in the courtroom.
- Chalmer's alibi was uncorroborated.

Postconviction Challenges

Chalmers filed an appeal claiming that the police lineup was improperly conducted. The Appellate Division of the New York Supreme Court ruled on July 18, 1990, that the lineup was properly conducted, and even if it were not, the victim's in-court identification was sufficient. The court affirmed Chalmers' conviction (559 N.Y.S.2d 27).

Chalmers applied to the Innocence Project to assist him in obtaining postconviction relief. Project lawyers secured the physical evidence and forwarded it to Forensic Science Associates (FSA) for DNA testing.

DNA Results

FSA tested samples of blood from the victim and Chalmers as well as from the vaginal and cervical swabs from the original rape kit. The first report from FSA, on July 8, 1994, showed the results from tests of the victim's blood and the two swabs. The second report, dated July 26, 1994, stated that Chalmers could be eliminated as the source of the semen on the two swabs on the basis of differences in three polymarker genes (see appendix for results).

Conclusion

Chalmers' conviction was vacated and charges were dismissed on January 31, 1995. The related larceny charges were dismissed in April 1995. Chalmers served 8 years of his sentence.

Ronald Cotton (Burlington, North Carolina)

Factual Background

In two separate incidents in July 1984, an assailant broke into an apartment, severed phone wires, sexually assaulted a woman, and searched through her belongings, taking money and other items.

On August 1, 1984, Ronald Cotton was arrested for the rapes. In January 1985, Cotton was convicted by a jury of one count of rape and one count of burglary. In a second trial, in November 1987, Cotton was convicted of both rapes and two counts of burglary. An Alamance County Superior Court sentenced Cotton to life plus 54 years.

Prosecutor's Evidence at Trial

Cotton's alibi was supported by family members. The jury was not allowed to hear evidence that the second victim failed to pick Cotton out of either a photo array or a police lineup. The prosecution based its case on several points:

- A photo identification was made by one of the victims.
- A police lineup identification was made by one of the victims.
- A flashlight in Cotton's home resembled the one used by the assailant.
- Rubber from Cotton's tennis shoe was consistent with rubber found at one of the crime scenes.

Postconviction Challenges

Cotton's attorney filed an appeal. The North Carolina Supreme Court overturned the conviction because the second victim had picked another man out of the lineup and the trial court did not allow this evidence to be heard by the jury.

In November 1987 Cotton was retried, this time for both rapes. The second victim had decided that Cotton was the assailant. Before the second trial, a man in prison, who had been convicted for crimes similar to these assaults, stated to another inmate that he had committed Cotton's crimes. The superior court judge refused to allow this information into evidence, and Cotton was convicted of both rapes and sentenced to life.

The next year Cotton's appellate defender filed a brief that did not argue the failure to admit the second suspect's confession. The conviction was affirmed. In 1994 two new lawyers, at the request of the chief appellate defender, took over Cotton's defense. They filed a motion for appropriate relief on the grounds of inadequate appeal counsel. They also filed a motion for DNA testing that was granted in October 1994. In the spring of 1995, the Burlington Police Department turned over all evidence that contained the assailant's semen for DNA testing.

DNA Results

The samples from one victim were too deteriorated to be conclusive, but the samples from the other victim's vaginal swab and underwear were submitted to PCR testing and showed no match to Cotton. At the defense attorneys' request, the results were sent to the State Bureau of Investigation's DNA data base containing the DNA patterns of convicted, violent felons in North Carolina prisons. The State's data base showed a match with the convict who had earlier confessed to the crime.

Conclusion

After Cotton's attorneys received the DNA test results in May 1995, they contacted the district attorney, who joined the defense attorneys in the motion to dismiss the charges. On June 30, 1995, Cotton was officially cleared of all charges and released from prison. In July 1995 the governor of North Carolina officially pardoned Cotton, making him eligible for $5,000 compensation from the State. Cotton had served $10^1/_2$ years of his sentence.

Rolando Cruz and Alejandro Hernandez (Chicago, Illinois)

Factual Background

On February 25, 1983, a 10-year-old girl was kidnaped from her home, raped, and bludgeoned to death. Her body was found several days later in a wooded area. An autopsy showed she had died from several blows to the head, and her body evidenced a broken nose, postmortem scratches, and sexual assault. Two weeks later an anonymous tip led sheriff's detectives to Hernandez. He allegedly made statements that he knew the men involved in the crime but that he was not one of the perpetrators. On the basis of his statements, Hernandez was arrested on March 6, 1984.

Several days later, the detectives spoke with Cruz, who was an acquaintance of Hernandez. Cruz allegedly reported "visions" to the police—visions whose details were similar to those associated with the crime. Cruz was indicted on March 9, 1984, on the basis of those statements.

In 1985, in a DuPage County Circuit Court, Rolando Cruz and Alejandro Hernandez were jointly tried, convicted, and sentenced to death for kidnaping, rape, and murder. A jury was unable to reach a verdict on a third codefendant.

Prosecutor's Evidence at Trial

The prosecution based its case on several points:

- Several law enforcement officers testified that Cruz and Hernandez made incriminating statements.
- Several witnesses testified that Cruz and Hernandez admitted to having intimate knowledge of the crime.
- Cruz's alleged "dream visions" of the murder, though not tape recorded, were admitted into evidence on the basis of the testimony of sheriff's detectives.
- The alibi defenses of the two men were not aggressively pursued.
- The Hernandez defense also contended that any inculpatory statements by him against others were made to collect a $10,000 reward.

Postconviction Challenges

After an appeal by Cruz, the Illinois Supreme Court ruled that Cruz was "denied a fair trial by reason of introduction of admissions of codefendants" (521 N.E.2d 18). The court ruled on January 19, 1988, that the three men should have been tried separately when it was clear that the prosecution was going to use inculpatory statements by defendants as evidence against one another. The case was reversed and remanded to the DuPage Circuit Court. The Illinois Supreme Court essentially made the same ruling on Hernandez's appeal (521 N.E.2d 25) on January 19, 1988.

Cruz was again convicted by a jury in a DuPage County Circuit Court, and he appealed. The Illinois Supreme Court initially affirmed the circuit court's decision, but, in view of many amicus curiae briefs, the court agreed to look at Cruz's conviction again. This time, on July 14, 1994, the court reversed the decision of the circuit court (643 N.E.2d 636). The reversal was largely based on statements made by another man, Brian Dugan, a convicted rapist-murderer, who claimed to have committed the crime alone. Dugan's confession was made through hypothetical statements during a plea bargain for other crimes, so the confession could not be used against him.

Hernandez's second conviction, in a separate appeal, was also reversed and remanded. He was convicted a third time by a jury, and this conviction, too, was overturned.

DNA Results

In September 1995 DNA tests showed that neither Cruz nor Hernandez were the contributors of the semen found at the crime scene. Tests also determined that Brian Dugan could not be eliminated as a potential contributor. Prosecutors contended that the DNA evidence showed only that Cruz and Hernandez were not the rapists, but they could still have been present at the crime. Cruz's new defense team decided on a bench trial. Hernandez awaited a fourth jury trial.

Conclusion

Before the judge gave a directed verdict in the Cruz case, a sheriff's department lieutenant recanted testimony he had provided in previous trials. In the earlier trials, the lieutenant provided corroborating testimony that two of his detectives told him immediately about Cruz's dream-vision statements. At Cruz's latest trial, however, the lieutenant said he was in Florida on the day of the supposed conversations and could not have spoken to anyone about Cruz's statements. On November 3, 1995, a DuPage County judge acquitted Cruz on the basis of the recanted testimony, the DNA evidence, and the lack of any substantiated evidence against Cruz. Rolando Cruz served 11 years on death row.

Hernandez's case was also dismissed, and he was set free. He served 11 years on death row. Brian Dugan has not been charged with the murder. He has refused to testify about the case unless he is granted death-penalty immunity.

Charles Dabbs (Westchester County, New York)

Factual Background

Early on the morning of August 12, 1982, the victim was walking home when she was assaulted from behind. She was forcibly dragged into an alley between a warehouse and another building. The assailant dropped the victim down a flight of stairs, and she lost consciousness. When she awoke, she saw two other men with the original assailant. One of the attackers held the woman's legs, one held her arms, and the third raped her. She was able to identify only the face of the man who raped her (allegedly Dabbs). The alleged accomplices were never located.

Charles Dabbs was convicted of first-degree rape by a jury in a Westchester County Court on April 10, 1984. He was ordered to serve 12½ to 20 years in prison.

Prosecutor's Evidence at Trial

The prosecution based its case on several points:

- The victim was able to identify Dabbs because they are distant cousins.
- The victim testified that the assailant wore a distinctive cap and had a distinctive laugh, which she stated were both similar to Dabbs'.
- ABO typing of a semen stain on the victim's pants showed the presence of the H and the B antigens; Dabbs is an O secretor whose body fluids contain the H antigen. This blood typing showed that Dabbs could not be excluded as a source of the semen.

Postconviction Challenges

Dabbs appealed his conviction, but it was upheld by the appellate court in June 1988 (529 N.Y.S.2d 557). On November 21, 1990, the Westchester County Supreme Court granted Dabbs' request for DNA testing (570 N.Y.S.2d 765). The court ruled that any preserved evidence was to be released by the county laboratory for testing by Lifecodes, Inc.

DNA Results

Lifecodes, Inc., reported that DNA tests of a gauze pad and a cutting from the victim's jeans yielded inconclusive results. RFLP testing was conducted, however, on a cutting from the victim's underwear. The DNA from the semen on the panties did not match the DNA from a blood sample submitted by Dabbs.

Conclusion

On the basis of the DNA results, Dabbs' attorney filed a motion to have the conviction vacated. The prosecution elected not to oppose Dabbs' motion, and on July 31, 1991, the Westchester County Supreme Court ruled that the DNA analysis was sufficient to indicate that the defendant was not the perpetrator. The prosecution moved to dismiss the indictment on the basis of the DNA results and the reluctance of the victim to testify at a new trial. The dismissal was granted by the court on August 22, 1991. The court's written opinion was published on November 7, 1991 (587 N.Y.S.2d 90). Dabbs served 7 years of his sentence.

Gerald Wayne Davis (Kanawha County, West Virginia)

Factual Background

The victim testified that on the evening of February 18, 1986, she had dropped off laundry at the home of Davis, a family friend. When she returned to pick up the laundry, she was attacked and raped by Davis on his waterbed. Davis's father, according to the victim's testimony, was present during the assault and made no efforts to intervene on her behalf.

In May 1986 Gerald Wayne Davis was convicted by a Kanawha County jury of kidnaping and two counts of sexual assault. The circuit court judge sentenced Davis to 14 to 35 years in prison. Dewey Davis, the defendant's father, also was convicted of abduction, first-degree sexual abuse, and second-degree sexual assault.

Prosecutor's Evidence at Trial

The prosecution based its case on several points:

- The victim knew Davis and identified him to police.
- The victim also made an in-court identification of Davis.
- A State police chemist testified that DNA tests could not exclude Davis as the source of the semen found on the victim's underpants.
- Police found a shoe and a jacket belonging to the victim in the Davis home.
- The Davises asserted an alibi that they did nothing while the victim washed clothes.

Postconviction Challenges

Both Davis and his father filed appeals. The appellate court dismissed one count of sexual assault and the kidnaping charge for both defendants. As a result, their sentences were reduced to 10 years each.

After an investigation of cases involving chemist Fred Zain (see also the Glen Woodall and William O'Dell Harris cases), many convicted persons were permitted to file a writ of habeas corpus if Zain worked on their cases. Davis filed such a writ based on the potential for falsified evidence by Zain and the possibility of exculpatory evidence in a new DNA test. The West Virginia Superior Court granted the writ on the condition that DNA tests be performed on the remaining trial evidence.

DNA Results

Davis's defense attorney asked for DNA tests to be performed on the original trial evidence. The judge agreed to the use of the Center for Blood Research (CBR) for testing. The results showed DNA markings from the victim and a man, but not from Davis. Prosecutors ran a second series of tests. They also excluded Davis as the semen source. DNA tests also were performed on Davis's underwear and bedsheets. These tests showed no evidence of the victim's DNA.

Conclusion

As a result of these DNA test results, the convictions were annulled and Davis was released to home confinement on March 16, 1994, pending a new trial. The prosecution, contending that Davis still could have raped the victim and not ejaculated, pursued a second trial. On December 4, 1995, a Kanawha County Circuit Court jury deliberated for 90 minutes before acquitting Davis of second-degree sexual assault and first-degree sexual abuse. All charges have also been dismissed against the elder Davis. Both Davises had served 8 years of their sentences.

Frederick Rene Daye (San Diego, California)

Factual Background

The crime occurred on the evening of January 10, 1984, while a young woman was walking from a drugstore to her car. One man (alleged to be Daye) opened the victim's driver side door, pushed the victim to the passenger side, and let a second man into the back seat. The two men, after finding only $6 in the woman's purse, stole the woman's wedding and engagement rings, a pearl ring, and her earrings. Then they forcibly removed her clothes and raped her. The two men dumped the victim on a residential street and drove away.

The two defendants were prosecuted in separate trials, and at Daye's trial the other defendant, who was known to a person who witnessed the car theft, pleaded the Fifth Amendment. A jury required almost 8 hours to convict Frederick Rene Daye of kidnaping, robbery, two counts of rape in concert, and vehicle theft. On August 14, 1984, the San Diego County Superior Court sentenced Daye to serve life, with the possibility of parole, on the kidnaping charge, and 14 years and 8 months for all other counts. He was ordered to serve his sentence at California State Prison-Solano.

Prosecutor's Evidence at Trial

Daye's defense at trial was mistaken identification. The prosecution's evidence included:

- Blood typing from a semen stain matched Daye's ABO blood type B.
- The victim made a photo identification.
- The victim and a witness to the crime made lineup identifications.
- Daye gave a false name and other misinformation to the police at the time of his arrest.

Postconviction Challenges

Daye appealed the conviction, claiming an erroneous admission of tainted identification evidence, ineffective counsel at trial, suppression of the out-of-court identification, improper impeachment with prior convictions, and instructional errors. The judgment of Daye's conviction was affirmed in appellate court on February 29, 1986. The California Supreme Court denied review of his case.

A statement by David Pringle, the other defendant in this case, was made to the San Diego County Superior Court on February 1, 1990. This statement indicated that Daye was not the other man involved in the crime; it also named the man who was with Pringle. The court appointed a defense attorney to investigate this matter. When no followup work was done by this attorney, Appellate Defenders, Inc. (ADI), helped Daye file a writ of habeas corpus petition. The petition, filed in June 1992, addressed both Pringle's affidavit and the lack of action taken by Daye's lawyer. Habeas relief was denied on August 11, 1992, and the case was remanded to superior court with directions to consider whether to vacate the appointment of Daye's attorney.

The court ruled that Daye was entitled to new representation, and ADI took over the case. In October 1992 Daye's attorney was notified that the original evidence from the trial was going to be destroyed. She filed for an evidentiary hearing to discuss release of the exhibits and DNA testing of any remaining semen stains. On September 17, 1993, the court of appeals denied Daye's request for an evidentiary hearing. The court, however, issued a writ making $2,000 available from the county for Daye to investigate the DNA issue and authorized release of evidence to an investigator working on Daye's case. Daye also received permission to seek habeas corpus relief after the completion of the DNA investigation.

DNA Results

The report from Cellmark Diagnostics, completed on April 21, 1994, stated that DNA from the left leg of the victim's jeans and Daye's blood sample were amplified using PCR and typed for DQ alpha using an amplitype HLA DQ alpha forensic DNA amplification and typing kit. A denim cloth cutting of the right leg of the jeans was also sent but produced no PCR results. The sperm fraction on the jeans produced results, but they were too faint for interpretation. The results excluded Daye as the source of the DNA from both the nonsperm cell fraction and the sperm fraction found on the left leg of the jeans (see appendix for results).

Conclusion

After the results of the DNA testing provided exculpatory evidence for Daye, his new appellate defender filed a petition for writ of habeas corpus on June 3, 1994. Her petition was based on the new DNA evidence, which was not available at the time of the crime or at the time of Daye's appeal. It was also based on the declaration of the other defendant that Daye did not commit the crime and that, in fact, he did not even know Daye. Daye's conviction was overturned on September 27, 1994. He had served 10 years of his sentence.

Gary Dotson (Chicago, Illinois)

Factual Background

On the evening of July 9, 1977, the complainant was walking home from work when two men forced her into the back seat of a car and raped her. She also testified that one of the men tried to write words on her stomach using a broken beer bottle. She was then pushed from the car onto the street.

In July 1979 Gary Dotson was convicted of aggravated kidnaping and rape. He was sentenced to not less than 25 and not more than 50 years.

Prosecutor's Evidence at Trial

The prosecution's case included the following evidence:

- A composite sketch of the defendant, which the complainant helped with, was prepared by the police.

- The victim identified Dotson from a police mug book.
- Dotson was identified by the victim from a police lineup.
- The State's expert serologist testified that the semen on the victim's undergarment came from a type B secretor and that the defendant was a type B secretor. (It was later reported that the State's serologist failed to disclose that the victim was also a type B secretor.)
- Testimony was presented that a pubic hair removed from the victim's underwear was similar to the defendant's and dissimilar to the victim's.

Postconviction Challenges

In March 1985 the victim recanted her testimony. She said she had fabricated the rape to hide a legitimate sexual encounter with her boyfriend. Dotson contended that the victim's recantation of testimony constituted grounds to vacate the original sentence. At the hearing on Dotson's motion for a new trial, the same judge from the original trial refused to order a new trial. His reasoning was that the complainant was more believable in her original testimony than in her recantation.

The governor accepted authority for the case and held a session of the Illinois Prisoner Review Board. The governor stated that he did not believe the victim's recantation and refused to pardon Dotson. On May 12, 1985, however, the governor commuted Dotson's sentence to the 6 years he had already served, pending good behavior. In 1987 the governor revoked Dotson's parole after Dotson was accused by his wife of assaulting her. The Appellate Court of Illinois affirmed Dotson's conviction on November 12, 1987 (516 N.E.2d 718). On Christmas Eve 1987 the governor granted Dotson a "last chance parole." Two days later, Dotson was arrested in a barroom fight, and his parole was revoked. In 1988 Dotson's new attorney had DNA tests conducted that were not available at the time of the alleged rape.

DNA Results

A sample of semen from the victim's underwear was sent to Dr. Alec Jeffreys in England for RFLP analysis. The sample was badly degraded, however, and results were inconclusive. Samples were then sent to Forensic Science Associates in Richmond, California. The lab performed PCR DQ alpha tests that showed that the semen on the victim's undergarments could not have come from Dotson but could have come from the victim's boyfriend.

Conclusion

The chief judge of the Cook County Criminal Court ruled that Dotson was entitled to a new trial. The State attorney's office, however, decided not to prosecute based on the victim's lack of credibility and the DNA test results. Dotson's conviction was overturned on August 14, 1989, after he had served a total of 8 years.

Edward Green (Washington, D.C.)

Factual Background

The incidents occurred on July 3 and August 5, 1987. In the first, a young woman was raped near a footbridge at a high school. The second incident occurred at the same location, but the woman fled and found a police officer. Police picked up Green in the area of the two assaults.

Edward Green was arrested and tried for rape and assault with intent to rape (in two separate incidents). He was convicted by a jury of the rape and acquitted for the assault/attempted rape. The jury reached its verdict in 3 hours.

Prosecutor's Evidence at Trial

The prosecution based its case on several points:

- The second victim identified Green in a "show-up" on the street.
- The first victim identified Green from a photo array and a formal lineup.
- Both victims made in-court identifications of Green.
- The blood type of the assailant was consistent with Green's.

Postconviction Challenges

After conviction but prior to sentencing, the defense moved to delay sentencing pending the results of DNA testing. While waiting for the DNA results, the prosecution opposed several time extensions, which were granted by the judge.

DNA Results

DNA tests were performed on an item of the victim's clothing and compared to the victim's and Green's blood. The report, issued in February 1990 from Cellmark Diagnostics, excluded Green as the source of the semen.

Conclusion

On the basis of the DNA results, the defense moved for a new trial. In a superior court hearing on March 19, 1990, the judge granted the defense motion. The U.S. attorney's office immediately moved to dismiss the indictment. Green remained in jail on unrelated drug charges after a pretrial confinement of 9 months in jail on the rape charges.

Ricky Hammond (Hartford, Connecticut)

Factual Background

In the late afternoon of November 30, 1987, the victim was walking on a dark street when she was pushed off the sidewalk by an assailant. The man forced her into a car in a nearby parking lot. He drove for about 15 minutes, stopped on or near a dirt road, and sexually assaulted her. The assailant then drove the victim to an area with which the victim was unfamiliar and told her he would kill her if she told anyone about the incident. He then let her out of the car and drove away.

Ricky Hammond was convicted of kidnaping and sexual assault in March 1990 by a Hartford jury. Before sentencing, Hammond filed two motions: one for a new trial and another for further discovery using DNA and blood testing of the vaginal swabs and smears that were in evidence. The trial court denied both of these motions and sentenced Hammond to a prison term of 25 years, suspended after 23 years, and 3 years probation.

Prosecutor's Evidence at Trial

DNA and blood analyses were performed at the request of the State prior to trial. The results provided exculpatory results for Hammond. The prosecution argued to the jury that, in light of the remaining inculpatory evidence, the physical evidence must have been contaminated. The prosecution's case against Hammond relied on several points:

- The victim identified Hammond in a photo array.
- The victim made an in-court identification of Hammond.
- The victim identified various details about Hammond's car, including the make and model, scratches on the body, a ripped child seat, and a wristwatch hanging on the gearbox.
- Hammond's alibi was uncorroborated, and he also had altered several details of his alibi when originally interviewed.

- Forensic examination of hairs found in Hammond's car showed they were consistent with the victim's hair.

Postconviction Challenges

Hammond appealed his conviction on three major grounds. Hammond claimed that (1) the trial court improperly denied his motion for a new trial because of exculpatory blood and DNA analysis, (2) the prosecution made improper statements to the jury and denied his right to a fair trial, and (3) the trial court erred in not allowing his posttrial motion to have further testing of vaginal swabs from the victim.

On February 25, 1992, the Supreme Court of Connecticut ruled that the trial court and prosecution made several errors with regard to the DNA and blood evidence. The court also ruled that the trial court was not aware of "the logical inconsistencies in the prosecution's case, the evidence suggesting that the chemical alteration of the assailant's DNA was physically impossible, or the absence of any evidence that the defendant's scientific tests were unreliable" (604 A.2d 793).

Because Hammond's motion was for a new trial and not for acquittal, the State Supreme Court remanded the case to the trial court for further proceedings.

DNA Results

The DNA results from this case were largely completed prior to trial. At the State's request, the FBI's DNA analysis unit tested the samples in May 1989. An FBI forensic analyst testified that the semen from the physical evidence could not have come from Hammond.

The victim's testimony indicated that she had not had sexual relations with anyone other than her assailant after putting on the clothes that were tested. Furthermore, blood tests performed by the State laboratory and the FBI lab revealed that the assailant had an A antigen in his blood. The victim, the victim's boyfriend, and Hammond all had type O blood. The secretions of blood type O contain the H antigen. Type O nonsecretors do not secrete the H antigen.

After the Connecticut Supreme Court's ruling, three more tests were performed on the vaginal swabs. Testing was not originally performed on the swabs because the State argued that it would be repetitive evidence. These results also showed no match to Hammond.

Conclusion

Hammond was granted a new trial and was acquitted. He had served 2 years of his sentence.

William O'Dell Harris (Charleston, West Virginia)

Factual Background

On December 16, 1984, a nurse was walking home from work when she was grabbed from behind and sexually assaulted. On July 25, 1985, Harris was arrested and charged with first-degree sexual assault. Harris was a juvenile at the time of the offense, but the State's motion to transfer the case to adult status was granted on May 16, 1986.

A Kanawha County jury deliberated for nearly 4 hours before convicting William O'Dell Harris of second-degree sexual assault. On October 18, 1987, Harris was sentenced to 10 to 20 years in prison, with 75 days credit for time served.

Prosecutor's Evidence at Trial

The prosecution based its case on several points:

- A sheriff's deputy testified that the victim had positively identified Harris as her attacker.
- The victim lived near Harris and originally claimed to have been acquainted with him.
- The victim identified Harris in a police lineup and made an in-court identification of him.
- Police serologist Fred Zain (see also Glen Woodall and Gerald Wayne Davis cases) testified that the genetic markers in the semen left by the assailant matched those of Harris and only 5.9 percent of the population.
- Harris's alibi, that he was with his girlfriend at the time of the crime, was corroborated only by her.

Postconviction Challenges

On November 10, 1993, the West Virginia Supreme Court of Appeals authorized special habeas corpus proceedings on any case involving the testimony of Zain (438 S.E.2d 501). One week later, Harris's attorneys filed a writ of habeas corpus, consenting to DNA testing of Harris as a condition of relief. On December 8, 1993, the State Supreme Court of Appeals issued the writ and remanded the case to the Circuit Court of Kanawha County for further proceedings. On December 29, 1993, the circuit court judge ordered prosecutors to release the trial evidence. More than a month later, the judge repeated his order.

The judge freed Harris to home confinement on $200,000 bond on June 21, 1994. At the same hearing, the judge again ordered the district attorney to release the evidence for DNA testing. At this time, the sheriff's department stated that all evidence from the trial had been lost. An investigator with the public defender's office later found a slide containing semen evidence at the medical center originally used by the victim.

On September 13, 1994, the judge held a hearing on a prosecution motion to reconsider his order of release of evidence and then ordered for a fourth time that the evidence (the slide from the medical center and a sample of the victim's blood) be released for DNA testing. Harris's attorneys filed a contempt of court motion on the prosecutors on November 1, 1994. During these hearings, the district attorney stated that the victim was being uncooperative about giving a blood sample but had sent the evidence slide for DNA testing on November 2, 1994.

DNA Results

On May 1, 1995, a report from Dr. David Bing of the Center for Blood Research Laboratories stated that DNA extracted from Harris's blood sample was inconsistent with DNA extracted from the semen on the evidence slide. Harris asked the circuit judge to dismiss the case against him. Prosecutors, however, requested that a second test be conducted by a court-approved laboratory, LabCorp in Research Triangle Park, North Carolina. This request was granted.

Conclusion

After the results of the second test also showed that Harris was not the donor of the semen on the evidence slide, the district attorney held a press conference on August 1, 1995, to state that Harris was innocent. On October 10, 1995, Harris's conviction was vacated. One month later, the court also dismissed the underlying indictment. Harris had served 7 years of his sentence and an additional year of home confinement. As an added note to this case, the detective who testified in this trial was later convicted for perjury.

Edward Honaker (Nelson County, Virginia)

Factual Background

In the early morning of June 23, 1984, a woman and her boyfriend were sleeping in their car on a rural roadside when a man approached, pretending to be a police officer. He ordered the two out of the car, brandished a gun, and ordered the boyfriend to run into the woods. The assailant forced the woman into his truck, drove to a secluded area, and repeatedly raped her. The police compiled a composite sketch of the assailant from the victim and her boyfriend. A woman was later raped 100 miles away, near Edward Honaker's house. She said the assailant resembled Honaker, her neighbor. Honaker had an alibi and was never charged with this second rape. The detective on the second rape case, however, took a picture of Honaker and showed it to the first victim and her boyfriend.

A Nelson County jury took 2 hours to convict Edward Honaker of seven counts of sexual assault, sodomy, and rape. The Nelson County Court sentenced Honaker to three life sentences plus 34 years.

Prosecutor's Evidence at Trial

The prosecution based its case on several points:

- The victim and her boyfriend picked Honaker out of a photo lineup.
- The victim made an in-court identification of Honaker.
- The truck that Honaker drove was similar to the one driven by the assailant.
- Police found camouflage fatigues in Honaker's house, similar to those worn by the assailant.
- Honaker's alibi, which was corroborated by his brother, sister-in-law, owner of his trailer park, and mother's housemate, was called a "put-up job" by the prosecution.
- A State laboratory forensic specialist testified that hair found on the woman's shorts "was unlikely to match anyone" other than Honaker.

Postconviction Challenges

Honaker made many written inquiries for any testing that could prove his innocence. Finally, Centurion Ministries (CM), a Princeton-based group that works to free the wrongfully imprisoned, agreed to work on Honaker's case. After CM discovered that some of the victim's and boyfriend's testimony was hypnotically induced, that the initial description given by the victim was inconsistent with Honaker's appearance, and that Honaker's 1976 vasectomy was barely mentioned in the trial (and not known by the prosecution's criminalist), the organization began working with the Innocence Project. Honaker's Innocence Project lawyers filed a motion with the State of Virginia to release evidence for DNA tests.

In the original trial, a forensics expert testified that sperm was present in the semen on the vaginal swab. The prosecution contended that the sperm was the boyfriend's, but they agreed to release the evidence to Honaker's lawyers. The Innocence Project, in turn, sent the evidence to Forensic Science Associates (FSA) for PCR testing.

The reason that FSA had to provide all the reports discussed below is that in June 1994 the victim claimed that she had a secret lover during the time of the original incident. This meant that DNA tests had to prove that one of the stains was not from Honaker or either boyfriend in order to establish Honaker's innocence.

DNA Results

The first report from FSA, on January 13, 1994, showed DQ alpha typing of a vaginal swab from the rape kit, an oral swab from the victim, a semen stain from the victim's shorts, and a blood sample from Honaker.

This report indicated that there were two different seminal deposits (the one on the swab and the one from the shorts did not match). FSA requested blood samples from the victim and the boyfriend. The report stated, however, that even if Honaker were able to produce sperm, he was eliminated as the source of sperm from both deposits (see appendix for results).

The second report from FSA was written on March 15, 1994; it included the boyfriend's typing and verified the victim's DQ alpha. The boyfriend could not be eliminated as a potential source of the sperm on the shorts. Honaker and the boyfriend were both eliminated as the source of sperm on the vaginal swab.

The Virginia State laboratory tested the second boyfriend and could not exclude him as the sperm source on the vaginal swab.

FSA then repeated the DQ alpha typing of all the evidence and typed five additional polymarker genes. Their report from September 26, 1994, stated that these additional polymarker tests showed that neither the boyfriends nor Honaker could have accounted for the sperm from the vaginal swab.

Conclusion

Virginia law provides that no new evidence can be presented more than 21 days after a trial, so a pardon from the governor was necessary in this case. In June 1994 Honaker filed a clemency petition with the governor's office. The Commonwealth attorney's office joined the petition on June 29. The governor signed a pardon for Honaker on October 21, 1994. He had served 10 years of his sentence.

Joe C. Jones (Topeka, Kansas)

Factual Background

Early in the morning of August 24, 1985, three women left a nightclub and sat talking in their cars. A man came between the two cars and ordered a woman out of one of them. He then got into the car with the victim and ordered her to drive away. After driving to a different section of town, the assailant asked the woman for her name and address. She supplied him with a phony name and number; then the assailant raped her.

Joe Jones was convicted of rape, aggravated kidnaping, and aggravated assault on February 13, 1986, by a Shawnee County jury. He was given a life sentence for the kidnaping charge, with lesser concurrent sentences for the other charges.

Prosecutor's Evidence at Trial

The prosecution based its case on several points:

- The two witnesses identified Jones as the man at the nightclub.
- The victim picked out a different man in a photo lineup but identified Jones when she saw him face-to-face.
- Jones was a member of the same club and had actually been there the night of the incident.
- The police found a pair of jeans that resembled those of the assailant in Jones' house.

In Jones' defense, a market employee testified that Jones was in his store at the time of the attack and was wearing different clothing.

Postconviction Challenges

An initial appeal by Jones was not disposed of before he combined that appeal with a motion of remand on February 2, 1987, with the Kansas Supreme Court. This latter motion asked for a new trial based on newly discovered evidence and ineffective counsel at trial.

The new evidence consisted of the following: another man who was later convicted of sexual assaults with identical modus operandi; expert witnesses who would testify that identifying Jones was unconscious transference on the part of the witnesses because they had seen him earlier in the evening and the identification was also weak because it was cross-racial; and a psychological exam showed that Jones did not have the capability to commit a violent act such as rape.

On February 13, 1987, the Kansas Supreme Court granted the motion for remand, but only in considering the evidence that the other man may have committed the crime. A hearing was held in which the other man denied any involvement with the crime, and the prosecution presented evidence that the other man's photograph was shown to the witnesses and they did not identify him as the assailant. The court denied the motion for a new trial.

Jones' attorney filed another appeal to the Kansas Supreme Court on the grounds that the defendant's homosexuality was not allowed as evidence at the trial, that the trial court refused to admit evidence about the other man, and that his client's Sixth Amendment rights were violated when the court limited the scope of his original remand. This motion was denied on March 3, 1989. Two years later, in 1991, the prosecution agreed to release evidence to the defense for DNA testing.

DNA Results

The samples and evidence were sent to Cellmark Diagnostics for DNA testing, but Cellmark was unable to get any readings from the evidence in the rape kit. Cellmark recommended Forensic Science Associates (FSA) as a laboratory that might be able to analyze the vaginal swab. The evidence was sent to FSA, which determined, in a report dated October 25, 1991, that the semen on the vaginal swab could not have come from Jones (see appendix for results).

FSA was asked to retype Jones' blood, and on April 13, 1992, FSA said that it had replicated its findings and Jones could not have supplied the semen on the vaginal swab.

Conclusion

On December 18, 1991, the defense submitted a motion for a new trial on the basis of newly discovered evidence. On July 17, 1992, a judge ruled that the DNA evidence was admissible. The court vacated Jones' conviction and ordered a new trial. The prosecution immediately stated it would not refile charges, and Jones was released that day. Jones served $6^{1}/_{2}$ years of his sentence.

Kerry Kotler (Suffolk County, New York)

Factual Background

A woman accused Kotler of raping her twice, once in 1978 and again in 1981. In the first incident, the victim alleged that she arrived home and a man wearing a ski mask raped her and robbed her of jewelry at knife point. She was unable to identify her assailant and reported only the burglary to the police. In the second incident, the victim again arrived home and an unmasked man was there. She said that the assailant claimed to be coming "back for another visit" and again raped her at knife point. He robbed her of jewelry and $343 and left through the back door. After 2 full days of deliberations, a Suffolk County jury convicted Kerry Kotler of two counts of rape in the first degree, two counts of burglary in the first degree, one count of robbery in the first degree, and two counts of burglary in the second degree. The court sentenced Kotler to 25 to 50 years.

Prosecutor's Evidence at Trial

The prosecution based its case on several points:

- The victim identified Kotler from a group of 500 photographs.
- The victim's identified Kotler by sight and voice from a police lineup.
- County laboratory tests showed that Kotler had three non-DNA genetic markers (ABO, PGM, and GLO) that matched those of the semen stain left on the victim's underpants.

Postconviction Challenges

Kotler brought a pro se motion to set aside the jury verdict prior to sentencing. In the motion, he alleged prosecutorial misconduct and deficiencies in the court's jury charge. The motion was denied on December 2, 1983.

In 1986 Kotler made a direct appeal to the Appellate Division. Among his claims in the appeal: erroneous admission of testimony, insufficient evidence to convict, and excessive sentencing. The judgment of conviction was affirmed on March 3, 1986.

On March 10, 1987, Kotler brought to the court a second motion to set aside the conviction. He based his motion on false testimony by a police detective, concealment of evidence, and improper cross-examination of Kotler regarding his prior criminal charges. This motion was denied on July 7, 1988. The court, however, ordered a hearing on whether certain documents had been concealed from the defense prior to trial. On January 8, 1990, after the hearing, the county court again denied Kotler's motion.

Upon hearing about DNA tests in September 1988, Kotler contacted the Legal Aid Society and asked for assistance in getting the tests performed. He secured funds from his father, and on February 15, 1989, the rape kit, the victim's underwear, and blood from the victim and Kotler were sent to Lifecodes, Inc. It found an insufficient amount of DNA for testing and returned the evidence. Another legal aid attorney, however, heard about Kotler's case and advised him to try Forensic Science Associates (FSA) in California.

DNA Results

In February 1990 all the evidence was sent to FSA. A PCR test showed that Kotler was not the source of the semen. The prosecution, however, posited that since DNA from both Kotler and the underwear yielded a similar allele, part of the semen could have come from a consensual partner and another part from Kotler.

Tests were then conducted by the Center for Blood Research (CBR) in Boston. They showed the same results as the first test. The defense then asked for a blood sample from the husband of the victim because he was the only sex partner the victim claimed to have had prior to the rape. After a sample from the husband was received by both laboratories, tests showed that he was also not the source of the semen. These results showed that the semen in the victim's underpants could not have come from either Kotler or the victim's husband. Both FSA and CBR issued a joint statement to the Suffolk County Court attesting to these facts on November 24, 1992 (see appendix for results).

Conclusion

On March 10, 1992, Kotler's attorneys filed a memorandum of law in support of Kotler's motion to vacate judgment. Their brief referred to the results of the original DNA tests as well as to the withholding of evidence by the prosecution, which included police reports showing that the victim's description differed from Kotler in age, height, and weight and that the victim's identification of Kotler was a "look-alike," not a positive identification. The district attorney's office filed a memo of opposition to vacate the conviction.

After the defense attorneys received the results of the final DNA tests, they went to the judge, who ordered a hearing on the results. The prosecution then agreed to issue a joint statement with Kotler's lawyers to vacate the conviction. The Court of Suffolk County ruled to vacate the conviction on December 1, 1992, and ordered Kotler to be released on his own recognizance.

On December 14, 1992, the prosecution sought the dismissal of all indictments, which the court granted. Kotler served 11 years of the sentence before he was released on December 1, 1992.[20] Subsequently, the chief prosecution expert who conducted the serology tests pleaded guilty to perjury charges that alleged he lied about his qualifications and training.

Steven Linscott (Cook County, Illinois)

Factual Background

On October 4, 1980, police found a woman dead in her apartment, face down and naked, except for a nightgown around her neck. Her head was covered with blood, and her body had many visible wounds. She had also been sexually assaulted.

Linscott was a neighbor of the victim and was questioned by police during a neighborhood canvass. He later remembered a dream he had the night of the murder, which seemed to parallel the incident. After reporting his dream to police, he gave several recorded interviews with police officers. He also gave saliva, blood, and hair samples to police.

Steven Linscott was arrested for murder and rape on November 25, 1980. In Cook County a circuit court jury took 10 hours to convict Linscott of murder and acquit him of rape. The judge sentenced Linscott to 40 years in prison.

Prosecutor's Evidence at Trial

The prosecution based its case against Linscott on several points:

---

[20] According to an April 9, 1996, *New York Times* account, Kotler was arraigned April 8, 1996, in Suffolk County, New York, on charges of first-degree rape and second-degree kidnaping. The charges stem from an alleged sexual assault on August 12, 1995, and the results of DNA tests on evidence taken from the victim's clothing.

- The dream that Linscott reported to police contained elements similar to those of the crime, including the following:
  1) The victim was beaten repeatedly both in the dream and in actuality.
  2) The victim was beaten in a downward motion both in the dream and in the actual crime.
  3) The weapon, in the dream, was long and thin; the actual weapon was a tire iron.
  4) The victim in the dream died passively; the actual victim was found with her hands formed in an "ommudra" sign used by Hindus to signify a passive acceptance of death.
- The results of blood-typing tests that showed that the semen from the crime scene could have come from Linscott.
- The results of head and pubic hair analyses showed that hairs found at the scene were "consistent" with Linscott's hair.

Postconviction Challenges

Linscott appealed, and on August 7, 1985, the Appellate Court of Illinois overturned the conviction (482 N.E.2d 403). The court ruled that the State did not produce direct evidence of Linscott's guilt and that his "confession" contained no voluntary acknowledgment of guilt. The prosecution appealed this decision to the Illinois Supreme Court. While the State's appeal was pending, the Illinois Supreme Court ruled on October 31, 1985, that Linscott could be released on bond. On October 17, 1986, the Illinois Supreme Court ruled that there was enough evidence to convict and reversed the decision of the appellate court (500 N.E.2d 420). The Supreme Court, however, also ruled that there appeared to be issues from the trial that were not addressed in the appeal, and the case was remanded to the appellate court for further review.

The appellate court was asked to review issues involving the physical evidence. The State's expert on the hair examination testified that only 1 in 4,500 persons would have consistent hairs when tested for 40 different characteristics. He only tested between 8 and 12 characteristics, however, and could not remember which ones. The appellate court ruled on July 29, 1987, that this testimony, coupled with the prosecution's use of it at closing argument, constituted denial of a fair trial (511 N.E.2d 1303). The conviction was again overturned.

Leave to appeal was again granted to the prosecution by the Illinois Supreme Court. On January 31, 1991, the court vacated the judgment by the appellate court, reversed the judgment by the circuit court, and remanded the case for a new trial (566 N.E.2d 1355). A trial date was set for July 22, 1992.

DNA Results

In preparation for the new trial, prosecutors attempted to bolster their case by submitting the physical evidence for PCR testing. The analysis by the Center for Blood Research (CBR) in Boston indicated that the semen could not have come from Linscott. DNA tests had been performed before the original trial, but the results were inconclusive and consumed all the swab material (see appendix for results).

Conclusion

On the basis of the results of the DNA analysis, the prosecutor decided that there were too many doubts to pursue the case any longer. On July 15, 1992, all charges against Linscott were dropped. He had served 3 years of his sentence and had been free on bond for 7 additional years.

Bruce Nelson (Allegheny County, Pennsylvania)

Factual Background

Two men stole a van and drove to a parking garage in the hopes of committing a robbery. They accosted a woman when she came into the garage and forced her into the van. The two men allegedly sexually assaulted the woman repeatedly, pulled out a knife, and choked the woman to death with a piece of cloth.

Those details of the incident are available only through the testimony of Terrence Moore following his arrest for the rape-murder. He confessed but testified that Bruce Nelson was the one who initiated the crimes and forced the victim into the van and killed her.

Nelson, already in prison on unrelated charges, was arrested. Police had Moore confront Nelson with his confession. During this confrontation, Nelson reportedly asked Moore, "What did you tell them?" Moore reportedly responded, "I told them everything."

Bruce Nelson was convicted of rape and murder in an Allegheny County jury trial. The district court sentenced him to life in prison for the murder and 10 to 20 years for the rape, to run concurrently with the life sentence.

Prosecutor's Evidence at Trial

Evidence was provided at trial that showed Moore's fingerprints on the victim's purse. Saliva from the woman's breast and bra was consistent with Moore's saliva. Saliva found on a cigarette butt at the scene was also consistent with Moore's saliva. Hairs found on the victim and her clothing were consistent with Moore's. The hairs, saliva, and fingerprints were not consistent with those of Nelson. The prosecution based its case against Nelson on two points:

- The testimony of Terrence Moore named Nelson as the initiator of the crimes and as the murderer.
- The statement by Nelson, "What did you tell them?" was entered into evidence as a confession.

Postconviction Challenges

Nelson filed a habeas corpus petition stating that the submittal of his confrontation with the other defendant, Terrence Moore, violated his Sixth Amendment right to counsel. Nelson also claimed a violation of his Fifth Amendment right to "restrictions on custodial interrogation of suspects who have invoked their right to silence." The district court denied his petition and his certificate for probable cause for appeal. The Pennsylvania Supreme Court declined to review the case.

The United States Court of Appeals for the Third Circuit granted Nelson's probable cause petition and reviewed his claims de novo. On August 17, 1990, the circuit court affirmed the district court's rejection of Nelson's Sixth Amendment claim but reversed its Fifth Amendment decision and remanded the case to the district court for further review (911 F.2d 928).

DNA Results

On remand, the prosecution obtained DNA tests to prepare for a new trial. The results of DNA tests excluded Nelson as the assailant.

Conclusion

On the basis of the results of the DNA testing, Nelson was cleared of all charges on August 28, 1991. He had served 9 years of his sentence.

Brian Piszczek (Cuyahoga County, Ohio)

Factual Background

In the early morning of July 29, 1990, the victim was at home alone when she heard a knock at her door. She looked through the peephole and asked the man to identify himself. The man said he was with the victim's friend, who was parking the car. When he said this, the victim thought she recognized his voice as belonging to a man named Tim or Tom, who had been in her house before. The victim let the man inside; he immediately pulled out a knife, cut the victim on the neck, breast, and stomach, and then raped her.

On June 25, 1991, after 1 day of deliberations, a Cuyahoga County jury convicted Brian Piszczek of rape, felonious assault, and burglary. The court sentenced him to 15 to 25 years.

Prosecutor's Evidence at Trial

The prosecution based its case on several points:

- The victim identified Piszczek from a photo array 2 months after the incident.
- The victim made an in-court identification of Piszczek.
- Piszczek testified that he had, in fact, been in the victim's house once before with the mutual friend of the victim.
- Piszczek's alibi was corroborated only by his girlfriend.

Postconviction Challenges

After Piszczek's conviction, a public defender took over his appeal. He filed an appeal on the basis of an improper photo identification process and ineffective counsel at trial (trial counsel never requested DNA testing, which was available at the time of conviction, and he was alleged to be ineffective in cross-examination of witnesses).

After the appeal was denied, the Innocence Project became involved. Its lawyers filed a release of evidence motion with the Cuyahoga County Court of Common Pleas. The request was granted on March 11, 1994. All evidence was forwarded to Forensic Science Associates (FSA) for PCR testing.

DNA Results

The report from FSA, issued on July 6, 1994, showed that PCR DQ alpha typing (as well as typing for five other polymarker genes) was performed on the blood of both Piszczek and the victim and on the sperm and nonsperm cell fractions of a vaginal swab, an anal swab, and a semen stain from a nightgown. The tests showed that Piszczek's DNA did not match the tested evidence (see appendix for results).

Conclusion

The day after receiving the DNA test results, the prosecutor's office asked a judge to overturn the conviction. On October 6, 1994, a Cuyahoga County judge declared Piszczek not guilty on all charges. Piszczek served 4 years in prison, including a period after his conviction was overturned.

Dwayne Scruggs (Indianapolis, Indiana)

Factual Background

On the night of February 1, 1986, when the victim was walking home from a bus station, a man came behind her, held a knife to her throat, and forced her to a grassy area near a highway overpass. There the assailant, while attempting to hide his face, sexually assaulted the victim and forcibly took $6 from her. After telling the victim to roll away from him, the assailant left the area on foot.

On May 13, 1986, Dwayne Scruggs was convicted of rape and robbery in a jury trial in a Marion County Superior Court. He was sentenced to serve 40 years on the rape charge and 20 years on the robbery charge, with sentences to run concurrently.

Prosecutor's Evidence at Trial

The prosecution's main evidence consisted of the following:

- The victim identified Scruggs ("with 98 percent surety") from a sex crimes file of approximately 200 photographs.
- The victim identified Scruggs a second time from a different picture and made an in-court identification of him at trial.
- The victim identified Scruggs' boots as matching those worn by her assailant.
- Scruggs acknowledged being familiar with the area where the rape occurred.

Postconviction Challenges

In August 1987 Scruggs' appeal was heard before the Supreme Court of Indiana (511 N.E.2d 1058). His petition was based on both a lack of evidence to convict and an "evidentiary harpoon" committed by a police officer who had testified before the jury that the victim had viewed photos of "individuals who have all been arrested for rape or a sexual assault." The jury was admonished to disregard his statement, but no mistrial was declared by the court. The supreme court affirmed the decision of the superior court.

On December 18, 1992, Scruggs' public defender submitted two motions on his behalf. The first was to amend the petition for postconviction relief. This motion stated that the defendant was denied due process of law when he was given a sentence that was not based upon the evidence in the case. Entering evidence of the petitioner's previous arrest for rape (for which he was not convicted) was also cited as a denial of due process. The motion also stated that the defendant was denied effective assistance of counsel at both the trial and appellate levels.

The second motion was for the release of all the State's evidence that contained biological samples of the victim for the purpose of performing DNA tests that were not available at the time of trial. On February 24, 1993, prior to a ruling on this motion, Scruggs' attorney filed a motion to allow production of laboratory reports that would analyze the evidence and blood samples from Scruggs. On April 26, 1993, the public defender also petitioned for blood samples to be drawn from the defendant.

The court held a hearing on all these motions on April 27, 1993, and ruled that the blood sample could be drawn and that the Indianapolis Police Department laboratory must release the vaginal swabs and slides. Those materials were sent to Cellmark Diagnostics in Maryland for DNA tests. The public defender's office paid for the testing.

DNA Results

The report from Cellmark stated that DNA from all the items sent were amplified using PCR and typed for DQ alpha using an amplitype HLA DQ alpha forensic DNA amplification and typing kit. The results excluded Scruggs as the source of the DNA from both the nonsperm cell fraction and sperm fraction of the vaginal swabs as well as from a bloodstain obtained at the scene of the crime (see appendix for results).

Conclusion

After verifying the results of this test, the prosecutor's office joined the defender's office in filing a motion to vacate Scruggs' conviction and sentence. On December 17, 1993, the Superior Court vacated both the sentence and the conviction and ordered Scruggs released. Five days later, the prosecution declined to prosecute in a new trial and asked the court to dismiss all charges against Scruggs. The court sustained the motion.

On March 28, 1994, the prosecuting attorney and the public defender filed for expungement of Scruggs' record. The next day, the court so ordered. Scruggs had served 7 years and 7 months of his sentence before release.

David Shephard (Union County, New Jersey)

Factual Background

On December 24, 1983, two men abducted a woman in the parking lot of a shopping mall. The victim was forced into the back seat of her car where one man pinned her arms and legs while the other drove. The driver stopped in a residential area where both men repeatedly assaulted her sexually. She was ordered out of her car, then the men drove away. The second assailant was never identified.

In September 1984 a Union County jury deliberated 1 day and found David Shephard guilty of rape, robbery, weapons violations, and terrorist threats. Shephard was sentenced to 30 years in prison.

Prosecutor's Evidence at Trial

The prosecution based its case on several points:

- The victim identified Shephard by sight and voice at his work.
- The victim heard one of the attackers call the other man Dave.
- The victim's purse and car were found near the airport building where Shephard worked.
- Blood test results showed that Shephard's antigens and secretor type matched those of the assailant.
- Shephard's alibi was uncorroborated and was punctured by the prosecution in cross-examination.

Postconviction Challenges

Shephard filed court papers in 1992 requesting that all evidence containing semen samples be released for DNA tests. The prosecution agreed.

DNA Results

The first DNA test indicated that one discernible semen stain on the vaginal swab from the rape kit did not match Shephard's. But the defendant was not vindicated because there had been two rapists. A second test revealed a second DNA sample that was too faint to read.

Shephard's defense attorney then asked the laboratory if any samples could be found on the panty liner the victim was wearing at the time of the attack. This test found two distinct DNA patterns, neither of which matched Shephard's. Subsequent testing, at the prosecutor's request, of the victim's boyfriend (the only person she was having consensual sex with at the time) showed that the boyfriend did not match either of the samples from the panty liner.

Conclusion

The Union County Superior Court ordered a new trial on the basis of the DNA evidence. Moments later, the prosecutor declined to pursue another trial, and Shephard was released on May 18, 1994. Shephard had served almost 10 years of his sentence.

Walter Snyder (Alexandria, Virginia)

Factual Background

In the early morning of October 28, 1985, a woman was raped and sodomized in her apartment by a man who had broken through her front door.

Walter Snyder was convicted of rape, sodomy, and burglary by an Alexandria, Virginia, jury on June 25, 1986. The jury recommended a sentence of 45 years, which the judge accepted and ordered Snyder to serve.

Prosecutor's Evidence at Trial

The prosecution based its case on several points:

- The victim identified Snyder as a person who lived across the street from her.
- The victim identified Snyder in a police station "show-up."

- Police found red shorts in Snyder's house similar to those worn by the assailant.
- Standard blood typing showed Snyder and the assailant were type A secretors.
- Snyder's alibi, that he was at home sleeping during the time of the assault, was corroborated only by his mother.

Postconviction Challenges

After Snyder's appeal of his conviction was denied, the Innocence Project agreed to defend him pro bono if his family could pay for any necessary forensic tests. In May 1992 prosecutors agreed to release the necessary evidence to the defense for DNA testing. The defense forwarded the evidence to the Center for Blood Research (CBR) in Boston.

DNA Results

On October 28, 1992, CBR issued a report stating that Snyder's DNA did not match the DNA in semen found on a vaginal swab from the original rape kit. The prosecution asked CBR to repeat the test, which it did for free at the Innocence Project's request. CBR replicated its findings, and the prosecution asked the FBI to look at the results. The FBI agreed with the methodology and the results in CBR's report (see appendix for results).

Conclusion

Virginia has a 21-day rule for a motion for a new trial based on newly discovered evidence, so the only recourse for Snyder was to seek a pardon from the governor. The Commonwealth's attorney joined the defense in filing a request for a pardon. Two months later, on April 23, 1993, the governor granted an absolute pardon; Snyder was released the same day. After being freed, Snyder petitioned the Alexandria Circuit Court to expunge his record. On January 11, 1994, the court granted his petition. Snyder had served almost 7 years of the original sentence.

Snyder's civil suit against the city of Alexandria is pending at the time of this report. In addition to wrongful imprisonment, the suit alleges that Snyder was beaten and handcuffed during interrogation and that police claims that Snyder confessed were false.

David Vasquez (Arlington County, Virginia)

Factual Background

In the early morning of January 24, 1984, a woman was sexually assaulted and murdered in her home by an assailant who had entered the home through the victim's basement window. The woman died from asphyxiation by hanging.

David Vasquez pleaded guilty to second-degree homicide and burglary (Alford plea) on February 4, 1985. He was sentenced to 35 years in prison. He had pled guilty to the crime after allegedly confessing to the crime and reporting details that were not released to the public. Vasquez, who is borderline retarded, later reported that he had only dreamed the crime.

Prosecutor's Evidence

In addition to Vasquez's guilty plea, the prosecution proffered the following evidence to the court:

- Two witnesses placed Vasquez near the victim's house on the day of the crime.
- Vasquez could not provide an alibi.
- Hair analysis of pubic hairs found at the scene were consistent with Vasquez's hair.
- A guilty plea meant that Vasquez would not be subject to the death penalty upon conviction.

Postconviction Challenges

There are no known postconviction challenges. Vasquez's defense attorneys, however, filed for a suppression of two of his confessions because they were issued without a Miranda warning.

DNA Results

The Virginia State laboratory, Cellmark Diagnostics, and Lifecodes, Inc., performed DNA tests on the evidence from several rape/ murders. All tests inculpated a man named Timothy Spencer as the assailant in rape-murders that were identical in modus operandi to the Vasquez incident.

Attempts by FSA to compare hair found at the scene with Vasquez's blood sample were inconclusive.

Conclusion

The Commonwealth's attorney and Vasquez's defense attorneys filed motions with the governor to grant Vasquez an unconditional pardon. The motions were based on the DNA tests of Spencer and an FBI report that indicated the Vasquez crime and the Spencer crimes were committed by the same person. The report also stated that the crimes "were not perpetrated by someone who was mentally deficient." The governor granted the pardon, and Vasquez was released on January 4, 1989. Vasquez had served 5 years of his sentence.

Timothy Spencer was arrested, tried, and convicted for two other rape-murders. He was never formally prosecuted in the Vasquez incident because he already had been sentenced to death. The United States Supreme Court denied Spencer's request for a new DNA test. On April 27, 1994, Spencer became the first person in the United States executed on the basis of DNA testing.

Glen Woodall (Huntington, West Virginia)

Factual Background

Two women, in separate incidents, were abducted at knife point in a shopping mall parking lot. Both times the assailant wore a ski mask and forced the victims to close their eyes throughout the attack. In the first instance, the attacker drove around in the woman's car, repeatedly raped her, and stole a gold watch and $5. The victim opened her eyes briefly to note that the assailant wore brown pants and was uncircumcised. In the second case, the man repeatedly raped the woman and stole a gold watch. This woman was able to note the man's boots, jacket, and hair color. She also noted that he was uncircumcised.

On July 8, 1987, a jury found Glen Woodall guilty of first-degree sexual assault of one woman, first-degree sexual abuse of a second woman, kidnaping both women, and aggravated robbery of both women. He was sentenced by the circuit court to two life terms without parole and to 203 to 335 years in prison, to be served consecutively.

Prosecutor's Evidence at Trial

The prosecution based its case on several points:

- A State police chemist testified that Woodall's blood secretions matched secretions in a semen sample from the evidence.
- A comparison of body and beard hair from the defendant was consistent with hair recovered from a victim's car.
- Partial visual identification of the defendant was made by one of the victims.
- One victim identified clothing that matched clothing found in the defendant's house.
- Both victims testified that the assailant was not circumcised, in common with the defendant.
- A distinctive smell about the assailant was noted by both victims and also was found at the defendant's workplace.

During the pretrial hearing, the judge denied a defense request for an "experimental new" DNA test of the defendant's blood and semen samples from the victims' clothing. Denial was based on defense inability to offer any expert testimony on the test's validity or reliability. After trial, the defense raised this issue again, and a DNA test was finally performed. The court held that test results were inconclusive.

Postconviction Challenges

On July 6, 1989, the West Virginia Supreme Court of Appeals affirmed Woodall's conviction (385 S.E.2d 253). Woodall continued to file motions to allow DNA testing of the evidence. He filed several appeal petitions and habeas corpus petitions with both the trial court and with the West Virginia Supreme Court. The State Supreme Court finally allowed the evidence to be released to the defense for additional DNA testing. This evidence was forwarded to Forensic Science Associates (FSA).

DNA Results

FSA conducted PCR testing of the semen samples from the vaginal swabs from the original rape kits. FSA concluded that the assailant in both cases had the same DQ alpha type and neither matched Woodall's type. These results were reviewed and confirmed in testimony by several laboratories and forensics experts, including Dr. Alec Jeffreys and Dr. David Bing of the Center for Blood Research (CBR). CBR also conducted its own PCR analysis and arrived at the same results as FSA (see appendix for results).

Conclusion

Woodall submitted a habeas corpus petition based on the DNA test results. On July 15, 1991, the trial court held a hearing on the petition and vacated Woodall's conviction. Other relevant evidence included secret hypnosis of the two victims and a romantic relationship between one of the victims and an investigating officer. The court set bond at $150,000 for Woodall and ordered him placed on electronic home monitoring. CBR continued conducting RFLP analysis and eliminated three potential donors as sources of the sperm. This was to counter the prosecution's argument that the stains may have come from consensual partners. The RFLP analysis also excluded Woodall, and the State conducted its own DNA test. The State's results also excluded Woodall, as noted in a report of April 23, 1992.

As a result of the additional testing, West Virginia moved to dismiss Woodall's indictment on May 4, 1992, and the trial court granted the motion. Woodall served 4 years of his sentence in prison and spent a year under electronic home confinement.

It is important to note that the State police chemist in this case, Fred Zain (see also Gerald Wayne Davis and William O'Dell Harris cases), was investigated by the West Virginia attorney general's office and the State Supreme Court of Appeals for providing perjured testimony in criminal cases. Glen Woodall was the first person whose conviction was overturned after Zain testified for the State. Over 130 cases in which Zain either performed lab tests or provided the testimony are being reviewed by the State attorney general's office. In addition, an investigation is ongoing in several Texas counties where Zain worked and testified as a laboratory expert.

Glen Woodall was awarded $l million from West Virginia for his wrongful conviction and false imprisonment.

GLOSSARY

Alleles. Alternate gene forms or variations, which are the basis of DNA testing.

Antigens. Any biological substance that can stimulate the production of, and combine with, antibodies. Variances in human antigens can be used to identify individuals within a population.

DNA. Deoxyribonucleic acid, which contains genetic material and whose shape resembles a rope ladder that has been twisted (the double helix). An individual's DNA is unique except in cases of identical twins.

DNA match. See *inclusion.*

DNA profiling. The process of testing to identify DNA patterns or types. In the forensic setting, this testing is used to indicate parentage or to exclude or include individuals as possible sources of body fluid stains (blood, saliva, semen) and other biological evidence (bones, teeth, hair).

DNA typing. See *DNA profiling.*

DQ alpha (DQα). An area (locus) of DNA that is used by the forensic community to characterize DNA. Because there exist seven variations (alleles) of DNA at this locus, individuals can be categorized into 1 of 28 different DQ alpha types. Determination of an individual's DQ alpha type involves a Polymerase Chain Reaction-based test.

Electrophoresis. A technique by which DNA fragments are placed in a gel and separated by size in response to an electrical field.

Epithelial cells. Membranous tissue forming the covering of most internal surfaces and organs and the outer surface of the body.

Epithelial cell fraction. One of two products from a differential extraction that removes DNA from epithelial cells before analysis of sperm DNA can be conducted. The other product is the sperm cell fraction.

Exclusion. A DNA test result indicating that an individual is excluded as the source of the DNA evidence. In the context of a criminal case, "exclusion" does not necessarily equate to "innocence."

Forensic science. The application of a field of science to the facts related to criminal and civil litigation.

Gene. A segment of a DNA molecule that is the biological unit of heredity and transmitted from parent to progeny.

Genotype. The genetic makeup of an organism, as distinguished from its physical appearance or phenotype.

Inclusion. A DNA test result indicating that an individual is not excluded as the source of the DNA evidence. In the context of a criminal case, "inclusion" does not necessarily equate to "guilt."

Inconclusive. The determination made following assessment of DNA profile results that, due to a limited amount of information present (e.g., mixture of profiles, insufficient DNA), prevents a *conclusive* comparison of profiles.

Marker. A gene with a known location on a chromosome and a clear-cut phenotype (physical appearance or observable properties) that is used as a point of reference when mapping another locus (physical position on a chromosome).

Polymerase Chain Reaction (PCR). A technique used in the process of DNA profiling.

Restriction Fragment Length Polymorphism (RFLP). A technique used in the process of DNA profiling.

Secretor. A person who secretes the ABH antigens of the ABO blood group in saliva and other body fluids.

Serologist. A forensic scientist who specializes in biological fluid analysis.

APPENDIX. DNA (PCR) RESULTS

A detailed laboratory report was obtained in 12 of the study cases; the results are reported here.

The following PCR results are the actual DQα types that laboratories found on evidence and blood samples. DQ α (pronounced DQ alpha) is one of several polymarkers that are compared in PCR testing. Each DQα type is similar to blood type (e.g., O, A, B). One can see that many times the victim's DQα matches the nonsperm fraction in a semen stain. One also can see that the sperm fraction of the semen stain does not match the type of the defendant (except Chalmers, where the difference occurred in polymarkers other than DQα).

Kirk Bloodsworth

Sample	DQα Type
Victim's blood sample	1.3, 4
Panties—semen stain (nonsperm fraction)	1.1, 3 (Trace 1.3, 4)
Panties—semen stain (sperm fraction)	1.1, 3
Bloodsworth's blood sample	1.2, 4

Ronnie Bullock

Sample	DQα Type
Panties (nonsperm cell fraction)	1.1, 2, 3
Panties (sperm fraction)	3
Victim's blood sample	1.1,2
Bullock's blood sample	4

Terry Leon Chalmers

Sample	DQα Type
Victim's blood sample	1.1, 3
Chalmers' blood sample	1.2, 4
Vaginal swab—sperm cell	1.2, 4
Cervical swab—sperm cell	1.2, 4

Note: The epithelial cells from the two swabs were too weak to get accurate readings. Although the DQα of Chalmers and the semen matched, three other polymarkers did not match.

Frederick Daye

Sample	DQα Type
Blue jeans—left knee (nonsperm fraction)	1.2, 4
Blue jeans—left knee (sperm fraction)	1.2, 4
Daye's blood sample	4, 4

Edward Honaker (results of three tests)

Sample	DQα Type
Victim's oral swab	3, 3
Vaginal swab (nonsperm fraction)	3, 3
Vaginal swab (sperm fraction)	3,4
Shorts (nonsperm fraction)	3, 3
Shorts (sperm fraction)	1.2, 4
Honaker's blood sample	1.2, 3
Boyfriend's blood sample	1.2, 4
Secret lover's blood sample	4, 4

Joe Jones

Sample	DQα Type
Victim's blood sample	3, 4
Jones' blood sample	1.2, 3

(Continued)

Sample	DQα Type
Vaginal swab (sperm fraction)	1.1, 4
Vaginal swab (nonsperm fraction)	3, 4

Kerry Kotler

Sample	DQα Type
Underpants (sperm fraction)	1.1, 4
Victim's blood sample	4, 4
Kotler's blood sample	4, 4
Husband's blood sample	2, 3

Steven Linscott

Sample	DQα Type
Vaginal swab (sperm fraction)	3, 4
Vaginal swab (nonsperm fraction)	1.1, 3
Victim's blood sample	1.1, 3
Linscott's blood sample	4

Brian Piszczek

Sample	DQα Type
Nightgown (sperm fraction)	1.2, 4
Nightgown (nonsperm fraction)	2, 3
Vaginal swab (sperm fraction)	1.2, 4
Vaginal swab (nonsperm fraction)	2, 3
Victim's blood sample	2, 3
Piszczek's blood sample	4, 4

Dwayne Scruggs

Sample	DQα Type
Vaginal swab (nonsperm cell fraction)	2, 4
Vaginal swab (sperm fraction)	1.1, 4
Bloodstain	2, 4
Scruggs' blood sample	4, 4

Walter Snyder

Sample	DQα Type
Vaginal swab (sperm fraction)	1.2, 1.3
Vaginal swab (nonsperm fraction)	2, 4
Victim's blood sample	2, 4
Snyder's blood sample	1.2, 4

Glen Woodall

Sample	DQα Type
Underpants of victim 2 (sperm fraction)	3, 4
Underpants of victim 2 (nonsperm fraction)	1.2, 3
Denim skirt of victim 1 (sperm fraction)	3, 4
Denim skirt of victim 2 (nonsperm fraction)	1.2, 4
Victim 1's blood sample	1.2, 4
Victim 2's blood sample	1.2, 3
Woodall's blood sample	2, 3

End Notes for Section I

[1] "Science is the search for truth—it is not a game in which one tries to beat his opponent, to do harm to others."—Linus Pauling, 1958. Cited in Beck, Emily Morison (ed.), *Familiar Quotations*, Boston: Little, Brown and Company, 1980.

[2] Keynote address by Attorney General Janet Reno before the American Academy of Forensic Sciences, Nashville, Tennessee, February 21, 1996.

[3] For articles debating the forensic use of DNA technology, see Thompson, William, "Evaluating the Admissibility of New Genetic Identification Tests: Lessons from the DNA War," *The Journal of Criminal Law & Criminology*, 84, 1 (1993):22–104; Harmon, Rockne, "Legal

Criticisms of DNA Typing: Where's the Beef?" *The Journal of Criminal Law & Criminology*, 84, 1 (1993):175–188; and Neufeld, Peter, "Have You No Sense of Decency?" *The Journal of Criminal Law & Criminology*, 84, 1 (1993):189–202.

[4] The study's results have been reviewed by many persons, including those involved in a peer review process. To date, no one has identified additional cases that, as of the study's completion in February 1996, are the type examined in this report.

[5] National Research Council, National Academy of Sciences, *DNA Technology in Forensic Science*, Washington, D.C.: National Academy Press, 1992:156. (Cited as NRC report.) Another reference source is McKenna, Judith, J. Cecil, and P. Coukos, "Reference Guide on Forensic DNA Evidence," *Reference Manual on Scientific Evidence*, Federal Judicial Center (1994). This guide has a useful glossary of terms at p. 323.

[6] Jeffreys, Alec J., Victoria Wilson, and Swee Lay Thein, "Hypervariable 'Minisatellite' Regions in Human Nature," *Nature*, 314 (1985):67; "Individual-Specific 'Fingerprints' of Human DNA," *Nature*, 316 (1985):76.

[7] The first reported use of DNA identification was in a noncriminal setting to prove a familial relationship. A Ghanaian boy was refused entry into the United Kingdom (U.K.) for lack of proof that he was the son of a woman who had the right of settlement in the U.K. Immigration authorities contended that the boy could be the nephew of the woman, not her son. DNA testing showed a high probability of a mother-son relationship. The U.K. Government accepted the test findings and admitted the boy. See Kelly, K.F, J.J. Rankin, and R.C. Wink, "Methods and Applications of DNA Finger-printing: A Guide for the Non-Scientist," *Criminal Law Review* (1987):105, 108; Note, "Stemming the DNA Tide; A Case for Quality Control Guidelines," *Hamline Law Review*, 16 (1992):211, 213–214.

[8] Gill, Peter, Alec J. Jeffreys, and David J. Werrett, "Forensic Application of DNA Fingerprints," *Nature*, 318 (1985):577. See also Seton, Craig, "Life for Sex Killer Who Sent Decoy to Take Genetic Test," *The Times* (London) (January 23, 1988):3. A popular account of this case, *The Blooding*, was written by crime novelist Joseph Wambaugh, New York, N.Y.: William Morrow & Co., Inc., 1989.

[9] Bureau of Justice Statistics, "Forensic DNA Analysis: Issues," Washington, D.C.: U.S. Department of Justice, Bureau of Justice Statistics, June 1991, at 4, note 8.

[10] The admissibility of the DNA evidence was upheld by the intermediate appeals court, which cited the uncontroverted testimony of the State's expert witnesses. *State* v. *Andrews*, 533 So.2d 841 (Dist. Ct. App. 1989). See also Office of Technology Assessment, Congress of the United States, *Genetic Witness: Forensic Uses of DNA Tests*, Washington, D.C.: July 1990.

[11] 385 S.E.2d 253 (W. Va. 1989).

[12] 384 S.E.2d 775 (1989). Additional court appeals by Spencer were rejected by the Virginia Supreme Court at 384 S.E.2d 785 (1989); 385 S.E.2d 850 (1989); and 393 S.E.2d 609 (1990).

[13] Supra note 12 at 783.

[14] Id., at 797.

[15] 545 N.Y.S.2d 985 (Sup. Ct. 1989). Castro's case was never tried. He pleaded guilty to the murders in late 1989.

[16] *Schwartz* v. *State*, 447 N.W.2d 422 (1989).

[17] Id., at 427. The Minnesota Supreme Court further held that the use of statistical probabilities testimony should be limited because of its potential for prejudicing the jury. Id., at 428. The opinion was later modified in *State* v. *Bloom*, 516 N.W.2d 159 (1994).

[18] *Frye* v. *United States*, 293 F. 1013 (D.C. Cir. 1923). The test for the admissibility of novel scientific evidence enunciated in this case has been the most frequently invoked one in American case law. To be admissible, scientific evidence must be "sufficiently established to have gained general acceptance in the particular field in which it belongs."

[19] *Daubert* v. *Merrell Dow Pharmaceuticals, Inc.*, 113 S.Ct. 2786 (1993). The Supreme Court used this civil case to articulate new standards for interpreting the admissibility of scientific evidence under the Federal rules of evidence. This standard, while encompassing *Frye*, allows a court to expand its examination to include other indicia of reliability, including publications, peer review, known error rate, and more. The court also should consider factors that might prejudice or mislead the jury. For the application of *Daubert* to DNA technology, see Sheck, Barry, "DNA and *Daubert*," *Cardozo Law Review*, 15 (1994):1959.

[20] This brief overview is not a treatise on DNA evidence admissibility in criminal cases. For more authoritative articles, see, Thompson, supra note 3; Kaye, D.H., "The Forensic Debut of the National Research Council's DNA Report: Population Structure, Ceiling Frequencies and the Need for Numbers," *Jurimetrics Journal*, 34, 4 (1994):369–382; Comments, "Admissibility of DNA Statistical Data: A Proliferation of Misconception," *California Western Law Review*, 30 (1993):145–178.

[21] National Research Council, National Academy of Sciences, *The Evaluation of Forensic DNA Evidence* (prepublication copy), Washington, D.C.: National Academy Press, 1996:2.14.

End Notes for Section II

[1] Matter of West Virginia State Police Crime Laboratory, 438 S.E.2nd 501, 503 (W.Va. 1993).

[2] Id., at 504.

[3] Virginia Supreme Court Rules, Rule 3A: 15(b).

[4] Giannelli, Paul, "Chain of Custody and the Handling of Real Evidence," *American Criminal Law Review*, 20, 4 (Spring 1983):527–568.

End Notes for Section III

[1] This report does not discuss the issue of government misconduct because it is not particularized to the use of DNA technology. Beyond the limited instances noted in this report, enough examples of government misconduct in the criminal justice system exist in the popular media for government officials to be well aware of the problem.

[2] *Commonwealth* v. *Brison*, 618 A.2d 420, 425 (Pa. Super. 1992).

[3] *Neil* v. *Biggers*, 409 U.S. 188, 199–200 (1972) (factors include accuracy of the witness' prior description of the defendant, opportunity to view the defendant at the time of the crime, level of certainty demonstrated, witness' degree of attention, and time between the crime and the confrontation).

[4] Loftus, Elizabeth, and D. Fishman, "Expert Psychological Testimony on Eyewitness Identification," *Law and Psychology Review*, 4 (1978):87–103 (lack of reliability on cross-racial identification); Loftus, Elizabeth, and W. Wagenaar, "Ten Cases of Eyewitness Identification: Logical and Procedural Problems," *Journal of Criminal Justice*, 18 (1990):291–319 (witnesses can be induced to point to the suspect after subtle suggestion on

the part of the investigator); and Cutler, Brian, et al., "The Reliability of Eyewitness Identification: The Role of System and Estimator Variables," *Law and Human Behavior*, 11, 3 (1987):233–258 (level of stress experienced during crime may affect identification).

[5] "DNA Testing Turns a Corner as Forensic Tool," *Law Enforcement News* (October 15, 1995):10.

[6] Loftus, Elizabeth, and N. Schneider, "Judicial Reactions to Expert Testimony Concerning Eyewitness Reliability," *UMKC Law Review*, 56, 1 (1987):1–45; and Handberg, Roger, "Expert Testimony on Eyewitness Identification: A New Pair of Glasses for the Jury," *American Criminal Law Review*, 32, 4 (Summer 1995):1013–1064.

[7] *Williamson* v. *Reynolds*, 904 F. Supp. 1529 (E.D. Okl. 1995).

[8] Id. at 1558. The National Research Council report, *DNA Technology in Forensic Science*, notes that, in contrast to microscopic hair comparison, with the advent of DNA technology, the use of hair as an individual identifier will become more common. National Research Council, National Academy of Sciences, *DNA Technology in Forensic Science*, Washington, D.C.: National Academy Press, 1992:158.

[9] *DNA Technology in Forensic Science*, supra note 8, at 145–146.

[10] Id., at 16. In its 1996 DNA report, *The Evaluation of Forensic DNA Technology* (National Academy Press, Washington, D.C.), the National Research Council reaffirmed this position (page 3.12). The DNA Identification Act of 1994 (Public Law 103–322) also provides for a DNA advisory board to set standards for DNA testing.

[11] Telephone conversation with Manuel Valdez, treasurer, American Society of Crime Laboratory Directors, March 8, 1996. (More than 100 public laboratories perform DNA tests.)

[12] See "Oops! We Forgot to Put It in the Refrigerator: DNA Identification and the State's Duty to Preserve Evidence," *The John Marshall Law Review*, 25 (1992):809–836.

[13] *Arizona* v. *Youngblood*, 109 S. Ct. 333, 337 (1988). The Supreme Court also stated that "police do not have a constitutional duty to perform any particular tests."

[14] Supra note 9 at 160.

[15] Virginia Supreme Court Rules, Rule 3A: 15(b).

[16] An Oregon judge recently released Laverne Pavlinac and John Sosnovske from prison, where they had served 5 years after being convicted of murdering a young woman. The judge set aside their convictions because Keith Hunter Jesperson, a convicted serial killer, pleaded guilty to the murder for which the couple was convicted. See *The New York Times*, November 28, 1995:28.

[17] *Tuffiash* v. *State*, 878 S.W. 2d 197 (Tex. App. 1994). This case involved perjured trial testimony from Fred Zain, the State's forensic serologist.

[18] See *State* v. *Thomas*, 586 A. 2d 250 (N.J. Appl. Div. 1991); and *Commonwealth* v. *Brison*, 618 A. 2d 420 (Pa. Super. 1992). Compare to *People* v. *Buxon*, 593 N.Y.S. 2d 87 (App. Div. 1993).

[19] "Crime-Solving by DNA Dragnet," *The Washington Post* (February 2, 1996):A21.

In: Exonerated by DNA
Editor: Darrell Shaw

ISBN: 978-1-63463-963-7
© 2015 Nova Science Publishers, Inc.

Chapter 2

DNA TESTING IN CRIMINAL JUSTICE: BACKGROUND, CURRENT LAW, GRANTS, AND ISSUES*

Nathan James

SUMMARY

Deoxyribonucleic acid, or DNA, is the fundamental building block for an individual's entire genetic makeup. DNA is a powerful tool for law enforcement investigations because each person's DNA is different from that of every other individual (except for identical twins). DNA can be extracted from a number of sources, such as hair, bone, teeth, saliva, and blood. As early as the 1980s, states began enacting laws that required collecting DNA samples from offenders convicted of certain sexual and other violent crimes. The samples were then analyzed and their profiles entered into state databases. Meanwhile, the Federal Bureau of Investigation (FBI) Laboratory convened a working group of federal, state, and local forensic scientists to establish guidelines for the use of forensic DNA analysis in laboratories. The group proposed guidelines that are the basis of current national quality assurance standards, and it urged the creation of a national DNA database. The criminal justice community began to utilize DNA analyses more often in criminal

* This is an edited, reformatted and augmented version of a Congressional Research Service publication, No. R41800, dated February 25, 2014.

investigations and trials, and in 1994 Congress enacted legislation to authorize the creation of a national DNA database.

Federal law (42 U.S.C §14132(a)) authorizes the FBI to operate and maintain a national DNA database where DNA profiles generated from samples collected from people under applicable legal authority and samples collected at crime scenes can be compared to generate leads in criminal investigations. Statutory provisions also authorize the collection of DNA samples from federal offenders and arrestees, District of Columbia offenders, and military offenders. State laws dictate which convicted offenders, and sometimes people arrested for crimes, will have profiles entered into state DNA databases, while federal law dictates the scope of the national database. Increasing awareness of the power of DNA to solve crimes has resulted in increased demand for DNA analysis, which has resulted in a backlog of casework. Some jurisdictions have started to use their DNA databases for familial searching, which involves using offender profiles to identify relatives who might be perpetrators of crimes. In addition to solving crimes, DNA analysis can help exonerate people incarcerated for crimes they did not commit.

Congress has authorized several grant programs to provide assistance to state and local governments for forensic sciences. Many of the programs focus on providing state and local governments with funding to reduce the backlog of forensic and convicted offender DNA samples waiting to be processed and entered into the national database. However, other grant programs provide funding for related purposes, such as offsetting the cost of providing post-conviction DNA testing.

In the 1990s and the early part of the last decade, most of the debate in Congress focused on the scope of DNA databases, reducing the backlog of DNA casework, and providing access to post-conviction DNA testing. Most of the debate about the scope of DNA databases faded away with the enactment of the Violence Against Women and Department of Justice Reauthorization Act of 2005 (P.L. 109-162), which expanded federal collection statutes to include anyone arrested or detained under the authority of the United States. The act also expanded the scope of the national database to include DNA profiles of individuals arrested for state crimes. However, concerns about the backlog of DNA casework have persisted. In addition, new issues related to the use of DNA in criminal justice have emerged, including whether (1) DNA databases should be used to conduct familial searches, (2) sexual assault evidence collection kits (i.e., "rape kits") should be standardized, and (3) there should be national accreditation standards for forensic laboratories.

INTRODUCTION

Deoxyribonucleic acid, or DNA, is the fundamental building block for an individual's entire genetic makeup. DNA is a powerful tool for law enforcement investigations because each person's DNA is different from that of every other individual (except for identical twins). By analyzing selected DNA sequences (called loci), a crime laboratory can develop a profile to be used in identifying a suspect.[1]

DNA can be extracted from a number of sources, such as hair, bone, teeth, saliva, and blood. Because the human body contains so many copies of DNA, even a minuscule amount of bodily fluid or tissue can yield useful information. Obtaining a DNA sample is not necessarily invasive; it can be as simple as a swab of the inside of the mouth to obtain saliva.

State and federal DNA databases have proved instrumental in solving crimes, reducing the risk of convicting the wrong person, and establishing the innocence of those wrongly convicted. DNA evidence is used to solve crimes in two ways:

- In cases where a suspect is known, a sample of that person's DNA can be compared to biological evidence found at a crime scene. The results of this comparison may then help establish whether the suspect was at the crime scene or whether he/she committed the crime.
- In cases where a suspect is not known, biological evidence from the crime scene can be analyzed and compared to offender profiles contained in existing DNA databases to assist in identifying the perpetrator. Through the use of DNA databases, biological evidence found at one crime scene can also be connected to other crime scenes, linking them to the same perpetrator or perpetrators.

Early congressional debate on DNA testing centered on whose profiles should be included in DNA databases. In recent years, concerns have been raised about the backlog of DNA casework and access to post-conviction testing. In the future, policy makers may also focus their attention on other issues related to the use of DNA in criminal justice, including whether (1) DNA databases should be used to conduct familial searches, (2) sexual assault evidence collection kits (i.e., "rape kits") should be standardized, and (3) there should be national accreditation standards for forensic laboratories.

This report provides an overview of how DNA is used to investigate crimes and help protect the innocent.[2] It also reviews current statutory law on collecting DNA samples, sharing DNA profiles generated from those samples, and providing access to post-conviction DNA testing. The report also includes a summary of grant programs authorized by Congress to assist state and local governments with reducing DNA backlogs, provide post-conviction DNA testing, and promote new technology in the field. It also reviews select issues Congress might consider should it legislate or conduct oversight in this area.

BACKGROUND

Federal law authorizes the Federal Bureau of Investigation (FBI) to operate and maintain a national DNA database where DNA profiles generated from samples collected from people under applicable legal authority and samples collected at crime scenes can be compared to generate leads in criminal investigations. Statutory provisions also authorize the collection of DNA samples from federal offenders and arrestees, District of Columbia offenders, and military offenders. State law dictates which convicted offenders and persons arrested for crimes will have profiles entered into state DNA databases, but federal law dictates which profiles entered into state databases can be uploaded into the national DNA database.

Increasing awareness of the power of DNA testing to solve crimes has increased demand for DNA analysis, which has resulted in a backlog of casework. The demonstrated ability of DNA testing to generate leads in criminal investigations has led some jurisdictions to use their DNA databases for familial searching, which involves using offender profiles to identify relatives who might be perpetrators of crimes. In addition to solving crimes, DNA analysis can also help exonerate people incarcerated for crimes they did not commit.

The National DNA Index System (NDIS) and the Combined DNA Index System (CODIS)

As early as the 1980s, states began enacting laws that required DNA samples from those offenders convicted of certain sexual offenses and other violent crimes. The samples were then analyzed and their profiles entered into state databases. Meanwhile, the FBI Laboratory convened a working group of federal, state, and local forensic scientists to establish guidelines for the use of forensic DNA analysis in laboratories. The group proposed guidelines that are the basis of current national quality assurance standards, and it urged the creation of a national DNA database.[3] In 1994, Congress authorized the FBI to establish and oversee the National DNA Index System (NDIS). When the NDIS launched in 1998, only nine states participated.[4] Currently, laboratories in all 50 states, the District of Columbia, the federal government, Puerto Rico, and the U.S. Army Criminal Investigation Laboratory participate in the NDIS.[5] The NDIS contains the DNA profiles provided by federal, state, and participating local crime laboratories.[6] As of November 2013, there are 192 laboratories in the United States participating in the NDIS.[7]

DNA profiles generated by laboratories operated by local law enforcement agencies are stored in Local DNA Index Systems (LDIS). DNA profiles generated by state laboratories, along with authorized profiles stored in participating LDIS, are uploaded into State DNA Index Systems (SDIS). Each state has its own laws specifying which profiles can be included in the SDIS.[8] DNA profiles generated by federal laboratories, along with authorized DNA profiles in participating SDIS, are uploaded into the NDIS.[9] Federal law dictates which DNA profiles can be stored in the NDIS (see below). The NDIS allows participating laboratories to compare DNA on the national level while the SDIS allows each state to compare DNA profiles stored at the state level. Federal, state, and local laboratories upload and compare DNA profiles using the Combined DNA Index System (CODIS) software produced and distributed by the FBI.[10]

CODIS searches three indexes (convicted offenders, arrestee, and forensic) to generate investigative leads. The convicted offender index contains DNA profiles developed from samples collected from convicted offenders; the arrestee index contains DNA profiles developed from samples collected from arrested but *not yet convicted* individuals; and the forensic index contains DNA profiles developed from samples collected at crime scenes. CODIS searches across these indexes to look for potential matches (also referred to as "hits").[11] Matches can occur between either the convicted offender or arrestee indexes and the forensic index, thereby providing law enforcement with the identity of one or more suspects.[12] Also, matches can occur between DNA profiles in the forensic index, thereby linking crime scenes to each other and identifying serial offenders.[13] Matches between multiple samples in the forensic index can allow law enforcement agencies in different jurisdictions to coordinate their efforts and share leads. No names or other personal identifiers for offender and arrestee DNA profiles are stored in the NDIS, so when a match is made in CODIS, the laboratories that submitted the DNA profiles to the NDIS are notified of the match and they contact each other to verify the match and coordinate their efforts.[14]

DNA Profiles

DNA profiles entered into CODIS are based on 13 core short tandem repeat (STR) loci selected by the FBI.[15] Currently, the 13 STR loci used by the FBI are non-coding, meaning that they have not been shown to be associated with human attributes such as height, eye or skin color, or susceptibility to a particular disease.[16] Each locus has two alleles, and it is these 13 pairs of alleles that are compared to match samples in the forensic index with profiles in either the offender or arrestee indexes. The 13 core loci chosen by the FBI provide a high level of discriminatory power. The probability that two unrelated individuals would share all 13 pairs of alleles is estimated to be one in several hundred billion.[17] Two random Americans will, on average, share two or three alleles.[18]

It is important to ensure the quality of the DNA profiles entered into the NDIS. If the profiles are not accurate, they are of little use for making matches between forensic and offender or arrestee profiles. The FBI helps ensure the quality of DNA profiles included in the NDIS by signing memorandums of understanding with state laboratories whereby the laboratory agrees to adhere to the FBI's Quality Assurance Standards (QAS, see below).[19] Laboratories submitting DNA profiles to the NDIS must be accredited and audited annually.[20] Annual audits can be conducted by either an internal or external auditor, but laboratories must be audited by an external agency at least once every two years.[21] Laboratories that do not pass the annual audit can be prevented from entering DNA profiles in CODIS.[22] Currently, most labs in the United States are audited by the American Society of Crime Laboratory Directors and its Laboratory Accreditation Board (ASCLD/LAB) and Forensic Quality Services (FQS). In addition, DNA analysts must undergo semiannual proficiency testing.[23] DNA analysts who do not pass their semiannual proficiency tests are not allowed to enter profiles into CODIS.[24] Laboratories are also required to conduct two reviews of all DNA profiles before they are entered into CODIS.[25]

Currently, as prescribed by federal law (see below), only public laboratories that comply with the QAS can submit DNA profiles to the NDIS. However, public laboratories are allowed to outsource casework to private laboratories. All private laboratories that conduct DNA testing for public laboratories must be accredited, be audited annually, and adhere to the requirements of the QAS.[26] Public laboratories are required to conduct an initial site visit to each private laboratory it contracts with to conduct DNA analyses.[27] If the public laboratory signs a contract with a private laboratory that is longer than one year, the public laboratory must conduct an annual site visit.[28] Public laboratories are also required to review all outsourced DNA profiles generated by private laboratories.[29] The review by the public laboratory is in addition to the two reviews private laboratories are required to conduct per the QAS.

An offender or arrestee profile in a DNA database consists of 26 numbers representing each of the two alleles for the 13 STR loci, an agency identification number, a sample identification number, and an identifier for the analyst that entered the information.[30] However, most jurisdictions retain the DNA sample used to generate the profile placed in CODIS.[31] DNA samples are usually retained for quality assurance purposes, such as confirming a hit made using the NDIS, and it allows jurisdictions to retest the sample if new technology is developed in the future.[32] Privacy advocates are concerned that stored DNA samples include a wealth of genetic information that could be misused.[33] States and the federal government have sought to prevent the unauthorized use of DNA samples. Some states have criminal penalties in place for individuals who misuse DNA samples collected for law enforcement purposes.[34] Under current law, anyone who misuses a DNA sample collected under federal authority is subject to a fine of up to $250,000, or imprisonment for up to one year.[35] The number of offender profiles included in the NDIS has increased as Congress has allowed states to include DNA profiles from a broader range of convicted offenders and persons arrested for certain crimes to be included in the database. States have also amended their DNA collection laws to reflect this expanded authority. As shown in **Table 1**, nearly 11 million new convicted offender and arrestee profiles have been added to NDIS over the past decade. This is in part because more forensic profiles have been added to the NDIS as state and local governments have started to work their way through backlogs of forensic casework. As also shown, over 400,000 new forensic profiles have been included in the NDIS since 2000. Data presented show that the expansion of the NDIS has mostly been driven by laboratories processing and entering offender profiles. The additional offender and forensic profiles have increased the number of investigate leads generated by DNA databases. Since 2000, the NDIS has aided in the investigation of nearly 175,000 crimes. Data in **Table 1** indicate that most matches occur between forensic and offender profiles stored in SDIS rather than the NDIS.

Table 1. Number of Profiles in the NDIS, Investigations Aided, and Hits Generated by Searches of NDIS

Year	Convicted Offender Profiles	Arrestee Profiles	Forensic Profiles	Investigations Aided	Forensic Hits	National Offender Hits (NDIS)	State Offender Hits (SDIS)	Total Offender Hits
2000	441,181	—	21,625	1,573	507	26	705	731
2002	1,247,163	—	46,177	6,670	1,832	638	4,394	5,032
2004	2,038,514	—	93,956	21,266	5,056	1,834	12,482	14,316
2006	3,977,435	54,313	160,582	45,364	9,493	4,397	30,138	34,535
2008	6,399,200	140,719	248,943	81,955	14,364	8,561	59,184	67,745
2010	8,564,705	668,849	351,951	130,317	21,983	15,724	97,772	113,496
2012[a]	9,761,083	1,139,065	436,937	174,680	28,993	20,698	132,517	153,215

Source: U.S. Department of Justice, Federal Bureau of Investigation, *CODIS Brochure*.

Notes: Amounts shown are cumulative starting with 2000. In the most recent *CODIS Brochure* the FBI published data on profiles in the NDIS for every other year starting with 2000. "Forensic hit" refers to cases where a match is made between two or more forensic profiles in the database. "Offender hit" refers to cases where an offender profile is matched to one or more forensic profile in the database.

a. Through June 2012.

One limitation of the data in **Table 1** is that they do not describe how the investigations were aided, the outcomes of the investigations, or whether any of the hits solved the alleged crimes.[36] Database hits do not always generate a new investigative lead; investigators, if they have already identified a suspect and they know that the suspect's profile is already in the database, may enter a forensic profile into the database and wait for a hit to be returned before investigating further. In addition, not all hits generated by the DNA databases are probative; just because someone's DNA is found at a crime scene does not always mean that the person who left the DNA is the perpetrator. Also, it is possible that one forensic or offender hit might lead to several arrests or aid in multiple investigations. The data published by the FBI provide a measure of the output generated by the NDIS, but the "hits" and "investigations aided" metrics are poor indicators of whether DNA databases aided in resolving criminal investigations.[37] For example, the data provide no indication of whether the hits generated by the NDIS resulted in a conviction or how many investigations resulted in an arrest. A study of database hits in San Francisco suggests that there is a need for more expansive data collection in order to properly to evaluate the effectiveness of DNA databases.[38] The study measured the outcomes of 198 DNA database hits in cold cases[39] generated by the San Francisco Police Department Forensic Biology Unit between 2001 and 2006. The researchers report that 90% of the cold hits were probative and provided investigators with substantive leads.[40] Probative hits led to judicial resolution (i.e., conviction, guilty plea, or parole revocation) 40% of the time.[41] Another 28% of the cases involving probative hits were either awaiting jury trial or the investigation was ongoing at the time the article was written. The researchers note that they found that nearly 70% of the probative hits could result in some form of judicial resolution. There were varying rates of success for database hits for different types of offenses. Nearly 9 in 10 probative hits in homicide and burglary cases either reached judicial resolution or could be resolved. However, judicial resolution or potential resolution was lower for sex offenses (approximately 1 in 2). In nearly half of the cases where a probative hit was made for a sex offense, either the prosecutor (17%) or the victim (31%) declined to move the case forward.[42]

DNA Backlog

Delays in processing DNA evidence can result in delays in apprehending or prosecuting violent or serial offenders or it can result in wrongfully convicted individuals serving time in prison for crimes they did not commit. In addition, persistent backlogs can result in crime laboratories prioritizing DNA analysis for violent offenses, such as homicide or sexual assault, over other offenses, such as property crimes, or it can result in law enforcement agencies establishing policies stating that biological evidence is not to be collected for minor offenses.[43] Not analyzing or collecting DNA samples for minor offenses could prevent law enforcement from apprehending offenders before they commit more serious crimes.

Forensic Casework

In a February 2011 report, the National Institute of Justice (NIJ) published estimates of the forensic casework backlogs in state and local laboratories in 2005, 2007, 2008, and 2009 (presented in **Figure 1**).[44] Different methodologies used to collect the data and survey response rates differed slightly, but the data show a pattern: the backlog of forensic casework continues to increase as the demand for forensic DNA casework continues to outpace the crime laboratory capacity to conduct such analyses.[45] It is important to remember that data presented in **Figure 1** present a national picture of the forensic DNA backlog; it is likely that some crime laboratories have little or no backlog, while other laboratories have significant backlogs.[46] Data also show that the backlog of forensic casework is not the result of a glut of old samples awaiting analysis; rather, the forensic casework backlog is mostly driven by increasing demand for DNA analysis in new cases. NIJ reports that the growing demand for DNA analysis is increasing for many reasons, including

- a growing awareness of the potential of DNA evidence to solve cases;
- more DNA samples are being collected from property crimes;
- advances in DNA technology allow tests to be conducted on smaller samples of DNA;
- more DNA testing in old, unsolved cases where the evidence was collected before DNA testing became widespread; and
- post-conviction DNA testing.[47]

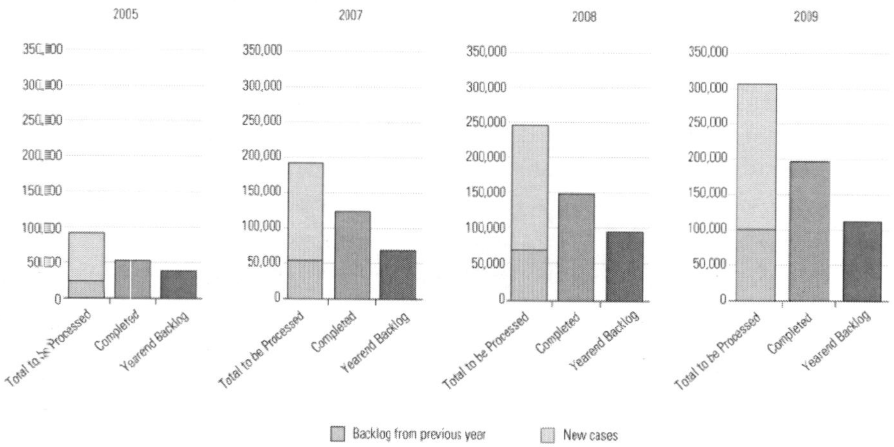

Source: CRS reproduction of a figure from the U.S. Department of Justice, Office of Justice Programs, National Institute of Justice, "Making Sense of DNA Backlogs—Myths vs. Reality," p. 3.

Notes: Backlog data for 2005 were collected as a part of the Bureau of Justice Statistic's 2005 Census of Publicly Funded Forensic Crime Laboratories. Data for 2007 were collected as a part of a NIJ-funded study of DNA backlogs. Data for 2008 and 2009 were reported by applicants for NIJ's FY2009 and FY2010 DNA Backlog Reduction Program grant solicitations. Data are not available for 2006. Data for 2009 is the most recent available.

Figure 1. DNA Forensic Casework: Supply, Demands, Backlogs.

Another contributing factor to the forensic casework backlog is the labor-intensive nature of processing forensic casework. NIJ reports that processing forensic evidence is time-consuming because the evidence must be screened to determine if, and what kind of, biological materials are present before DNA testing can begin.[48]

Convicted Offender and Arrestee Samples

In addition to the backlog of forensic casework, there is a backlog in the processing of samples collected from convicted offenders and arrestees. Backlogs of convicted offender and arrestee samples means that there are fewer DNA profiles in CODIS to match forensic profiles to, and this could result in a delay in identifying suspects in cases where DNA evidence was collected. Data collected by NIJ show that submission of new DNA samples from convicted offenders and arrestees increased between 2007 and 2009 (see **Figure 2**).[49] At the same time, the total number of convicted offender and arrestee samples analyzed decreased between 2007 and 2008, but the number of samples analyzed remained at approximately 1 million in both 2008 and 2009.[50] Therefore, the increased backlog of convicted offender and arrestee samples between 2008 and 2009 was the result of states collecting more offender samples, especially from arrestees, while the ability to analyze those samples remained flat. Data indicate that there are more convicted offender and arrestee DNA samples for laboratories to process compared to forensic samples; NIJ notes, however, that offender and arrestee samples are easier and faster to analyze because they are collected on a standard, consistent medium.[51] The standardized collection method makes it possible to use automated analysis on robotic platforms that can process approximately 96 samples and controls simultaneously.[52] This suggests that laboratories might be better able to process the backlog of convicted offender and arrestee samples if they increase their technological capacity.

Evidence in the Possession of Law Enforcement

One limitation to the backlog data discussed above is that they only include samples in the possession of crime laboratories. Samples from evidence still in the possession of law enforcement agencies and not yet transferred to laboratories are not counted as a part of the backlog. While there is no current count of the total amount of unanalyzed evidence in the possession of law enforcement agencies, one group of researchers that surveyed over 2,000 law enforcement agencies in 2007 found that law enforcement agencies had forensic evidence that had not been submitted to a crime laboratory for analysis in 14% of all unsolved homicide cases and 18% of unsolved rape cases.[53] The researchers estimated that nearly 40% of unanalyzed murder and rape cases contained DNA evidence.[54] The results of the survey indicate that there are many reasons why law enforcement agencies chose not to submit evidence for analysis, including that subsequent investigation may have shown that the evidence would not be probative; charges against an alleged perpetrator may have been dropped; or the suspect may have pled guilty.[55] However, data collected by the researchers also suggest that law enforcement agencies may not fully understand the potential value forensic evidence can have in generating leads in cases where they have not identified a suspect. Nearly half of the responding law enforcement agencies reported that they did not submit evidence for analysis because a suspect had not been identified. Also, nearly one in five agencies reported that they did not submit evidence because they felt it would not be useful to the case.[56] However, the survey does not reveal how many open cases with unanalyzed evidence would be solved or yield investigative leads if evidence were to be sent to the laboratory.

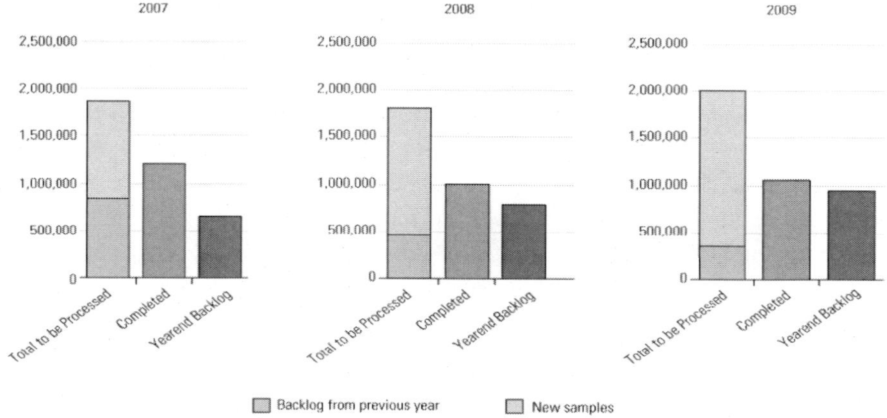

Source: U.S. Department of Justice, Office of Justice Programs, National Institute of Justice, "Making Sense of DNA Backlogs—Myths vs. Reality," p. 7.

Notes: Data for 2007 were collected as a part of a NIJ-funded study of DNA backlogs. Data for 2008 and 2009 were reported by applicants for NIJ's FY2009 and FY2010 DNA Backlog Reduction Program grant solicitations. Data for 2009 is the most recent available.

Figure 2. Convicted Offender and Arrestee Backlog Trends, 2007-2009.

Processing Time for DNA Analyses

While many policy makers are interested in the size of the backlog of forensic casework and offender and arrestee samples, another important consideration is the time it takes for laboratories to complete new requests for DNA analysis (i.e., turnaround time). Researchers studying the size of the forensic casework backlog in 2007 in publicly funded, accredited DNA laboratories found that 14 of the 145 laboratories (9.7%) responding to their survey reported that they did not have a backlog, meaning that they were able to process all requests for DNA analysis within 30 days of receipt.[57] However, nearly three-quarters (111) of responding laboratories reported completing DNA analysis requests within 119 days (four months) or less. Of the remaining laboratories, 24 (16.6%) reported that turnaround time was more than 180 days (six months) and another 20 (13.8%) laboratories reported turnaround times of 270 days (nine months) or more. The researchers found that the turnaround time for cases of violent crimes was, in general, shorter than the turnaround time for cases of non-violent crimes.[58] The researchers also found that the turnaround time for analysis of offender and arrestee samples tended to be shorter than the turnaround time for forensic casework. Approximately 30% of responding laboratories reported having turnaround times of 30 days or less for offender and arrestee samples.[59] Approximately half of all responding laboratories reported processing offender and arrestee samples within 90 days of receipt. However, one-quarter of laboratories reported turnaround times of more than 270 days (nine months) for these samples.[60]

Sexual Assault Evidence Collection Kits

There continues to be concern about the backlog of sexual assault evidence collections kits—also referred to as "rape kits." While there have been several estimates of the backlog in some cities,[61] NIJ reports that currently there is no comprehensive data on the number of unanalyzed sexual assault evidence kits in the United States.[62] NIJ reports that it is currently funding research to better understand why some sexual assault evidence collection kits are not submitted to a crime laboratory for analysis.[63] The backlog of sexual assault evidence collection kits has raised concerns that additional victimizations could have been prevented had the evidence from any given kit been tested and the perpetrator apprehended in a timely manner.[64]

Sexual assault evidence collection kits are collections of tools used by a nurse examiner or another trained professional to collect evidence during a forensic medical exam conducted after someone has reported a sexual assault and consents to the exam.[65] Many jurisdictions have developed their own sexual assault evidence collection kits, or they purchase them from a commercial vendor. As such, the content of a kit can vary from jurisdiction to jurisdiction.[66] In general, sexual assault evidence collection kits include (1) instructions; (2) bags, sheets, and envelopes for evidence collection; (3) swabs for collecting fluids or secretions that could contain the perpetrator's DNA; (4) a comb for collecting hair samples; (5) blood collection devices; and (6) documentation forms.[67] An exam involves collecting a complete medical history from the victim and completing a full-body physical examination.[68] This may include

- collecting blood, urine, hair, and other body secretion samples;
- photo documentation of any injuries sustained during the assault;
- collecting the victim's clothing, especially undergarments; and
- collecting any possible physical evidence that may have transferred onto the victim from the crime scene.[69]

In addition to jurisdictional differences in the content of sexual assault evidence collection kits, procedures for analyzing the evidence collected using the kit can vary from jurisdiction to jurisdiction. In some jurisdictions, all sexual assault evidence collection kits are forwarded to a crime laboratory for analysis.[70] In other jurisdictions, it may be months or even years before the kit is tested, if at all.[71] Some law enforcement agencies might not submit sexual assault evidence collection kits to crime laboratories for various reasons: the identity of the perpetrator was not in question from the beginning of the investigation, detectives identified the suspect through other evidence not included in the kit, or the victim chooses not to proceed with the case.[72] Also, some law enforcement agencies might have a problem working through their backlog of old kits because crime laboratories are operating at full capacity analyzing DNA evidence collected from current cases.[73]

Investigation of Leads Generated from Database Hits

While reducing casework backlogs can help generate new leads in cases without suspects (so-called "cold cases"), law enforcement agencies have to devote time to investigating the leads that result from DNA database matches. Data from a 2009 survey of 235 law enforcement agencies suggest that law enforcement agencies, particularly small agencies, might not have the resources to fully investigate new leads. The survey found that 37% of agencies surveyed had designated "cold case units" (i.e., groups of investigators who are responsible for leads generated from a match between an offender and forensic profile in either the SDIS or the NDIS).[74] In addition, the larger the agency (as measured by the number of sworn officers) the more likely they were to have such a unit. Over two-thirds of law enforcement agencies with 1,000 or more sworn officers reported having a cold case unit.[75] However, less than half of law enforcement agencies with 379- 999 sworn officers reported having this unit, and less than 20% of agencies with 378 or fewer sworn officers reported having such a unit.[76] Even if an agency reported having a cold case unit, the unit was typically small. Three-quarters of law enforcement agencies with cold case units reported that three or fewer staff members were assigned to the unit.[77] Law enforcement agencies that did not have cold case units reported that leads generated from DNA database hits were investigated when resources were available, which usually meant that investigators were paid overtime to follow-up on the new leads.[78] Data suggest that law enforcement agencies would expand cold case units if they had the resources. Surveyed law enforcement agencies were asked to identify, based on their agency's experiences, the resources they needed for DNA-related work. Two-thirds identified cold case unit staffing (both for staffing cold case units or paying overtime if the agency did not have a cold case unit) as a need.[79]

Partial Match Searching

Crime laboratories can use three levels of stringency—high, moderate, and low—when using CODIS to search for matches between an offender or arrestee and forensic profiles. Searches with high stringency require a match between all 26 alleles,[80] which, as discussed above, indicates that it is highly probable that the identified offender or arrestee was the source of the forensic sample. A moderate stringency search requires all available alleles to match, but the profiles can contain a different number of alleles.[81] Moderate stringency searches can be used to search for matches when the forensic profile contains a mixture of DNA from two or more sources, hence there might be more than two alleles at some loci. Low stringency searches require one allele at each loci to match.[82] Low stringency searches are sometimes required because a degraded sample might not have alleles at all loci.[83]

Crime laboratories can use low stringency searches to make partial matches between and offender or arrestee and forensic profiles. Partial match searching can be used for familial searching, which involves using DNA from known individuals in a database to identify relatives of those individuals as potential suspects in other crimes.[84] There is some debate about whether partial match searching is the same as familial searching. In some states, crime laboratories can release information on partial matches that result from a regular search of the SDIS or NDIS, but they do not consider these partial matches to be familial searches because they were not the result of a *deliberate* search of the database for partial matches between an offender or arrestee and forensic profiles.[85] Others argue that even if the partial match was not the result of a deliberate search of the database, it is still a familial search because it could implicate the relative of someone with a profile in the database.[86] Research indicates that there is a lack of transparency when it comes to policies regarding partial matches. In most cases where a state reports the results of partial matches, it is done without explicit statutory authorization, and in many instances the policy is unwritten or it is not available to the public.[87]

Familial searching is possible because of the way humans inherit genes. Close relatives especially parents, children, and siblings—who are genetically related are more likely to share alleles used for identification in CODIS than two people who are not closely related.[88] Two unrelated people usually only share a few CODIS alleles, but a parent and his or her child must share no fewer than 13 alleles since children inherit half of their genes from each parent.[89] Parents and children will most likely share between 14 and 16 alleles.[90] It is possible that two siblings will share between 0 and 26 alleles, but on average they will share 16.7 alleles.[91] Familial searching can be conducted by using low stringency searching, but low stringency searches can result in hundreds or even thousands of partial matches, none of which might actually represent a biological relationship. The probability that two unrelated people will share more than 13 alleles with at least one match at each of the 13 loci is about 1 in 2,000.[92] While this probability is low, there are over 8.6 million offender profiles in the NDIS, meaning that a low stringency search for a common genotype could generate thousands of partial matches.

The FBI has been reluctant to allow the NDIS to be used for familial searching without explicit legislative approval,[93] but in July 2006 the FBI issued a policy that permits states, at their discretion, to share identification information with other states in the event that a search of the NDIS turns up a partial match.[94] While the FBI's policy might seem to be at odds with the bureau's reluctance to allow the NDIS to be used for familial searching, a closer review of the FBI's definition of "familial searching" shows how the FBI could allow states to share partial match information without contradicting its stance on familial searching. The FBI defines familial searching "as a 'second deliberate search ... to identify close biological relatives of the perpetrator in the known offender database,' used only after an initial search of the database turns up no candidate matches."[95] The FBI's current policy allows states to share any partial matches; they do not have to be the result of a deliberate search for relatives of individuals with a profile in the NDIS. The FBI's policy means that states have the final say over whether to release identifying information in the case of partial matches.

FEDERAL LAW

While state law dictates whose profiles will be included in each state's DNA database, federal law provides for the collection of DNA samples from certain federal offenders for analysis and inclusion in the NDIS. Federal law also dictates which profiles included in SDIS can be uploaded into the NDIS. Federal law also states that agencies participating in the NDIS must meet certain specified standards. In addition, federal law provides for post-conviction DNA testing for federal offenders. The following section summarizes current federal law as it pertains to DNA used in a criminal justice capacity.

Quality Assurance and Proficiency Testing Standards

Under current law,[96] the FBI is required to issue (and revise from time to time) Quality Assurance Standards (QAS), including standards for testing the proficiency of forensic laboratories and forensic analysts, in conducting DNA analyses.[97] By law, the QAS must specify the criteria for quality assurance and proficiency tests to be applied to the various types of DNA analyses conducted by forensic laboratories.[98] In addition, the QAS must include a system for grading proficiency testing performance to determine whether a laboratory is performing acceptably.[99] Under current law, FBI personnel who perform DNA analyses must undergo semiannual external proficiency testing by a DNA proficiency testing program that meets the standards set in the QAS.[100]

According to the FBI, the QAS describe the minimum standards for a laboratory's quality assurance program if performing forensic DNA analysis.[101] The minimum standards cover the following areas: organization, personnel, facilities, evidence or sample control, validation, analytical procedures, equipment calibration and maintenance, reports, review, proficiency testing, corrective action, audits, safety, and outsourcing.[102]

Index to Facilitate Law Enforcement Exchange of DNA Identification Information

The Violent Crime Control and Law Enforcement Act of 1994 (P.L. 103-322) authorized the FBI to establish an index of DNA profiles (i.e., NDIS). Under current law,[103] the NDIS can contain the DNA profiles of samples

- taken from individuals convicted of or charged with a crime, or collected under applicable legal authorities (e.g., people arrested for crimes), except for DNA samples that are voluntarily submitted solely for elimination purposes;
- recovered from crime scenes;
- recovered from unidentified human remains; and
- voluntarily contributed from relatives of missing persons.[104]

The NDIS can only include DNA profiles

- based on analyses performed by or on behalf of a criminal justice agency or the Department of Defense (DOD) in accordance with available standards that satisfy or exceed the FBI's published QAS;
- that are prepared by laboratories that (1) have been accredited by a nonprofit professional organization of persons actively involved in forensic science and nationally recognized within the forensic science community, and (2) undergo external audits, not less than once every other year, that demonstrate compliance with the FBI's QAS;[105] and
- that are maintained by federal, state, and local criminal justice agencies or the DOD pursuant to rules that allow the disclosure of profiles only to other criminal justice agencies for identification purposes, judicial proceedings, criminal defense purposes, and, if personally identifiable information is removed, for research and quality control purposes.[106]

Under current law, the FBI is required to expunge the DNA profile of an individual who had a DNA profile entered into the NDIS on the basis of being convicted for a qualifying federal offense (see below) if the individual provides a certified copy of a final court order showing that the conviction was overturned.[107] Also, the FBI is required to expunge the DNA profile of an individual who had a DNA profile entered into the NDIS on the basis of being arrested under the authority of the United States if the individual provides a certified copy of a final court order that establishes that the charge was dismissed or resulted in an acquittal, or that no charge was filed within the applicable time period.[108] As a condition of having access to the NDIS, states must also have in place a procedure whereby the state will expunge a profile from the state's database based on the same conditions applicable to a profile being expunged from the NDIS.[109] Also, under current law the Department of Defense is required to expunge the DNA profile of an individual who had a DNA profile entered into the NDIS on the basis of being convicted of a qualifying military offense (see below) if the individual provides a certified copy of a final court order showing that the conviction was overturned.[110]

Collection of DNA Samples from Certain Federal, District of Columbia, and Military Offenders

Under current law,[111] the Attorney General is permitted to collect DNA samples from "individuals who are arrested, facing charges, or convicted of a crime or from non-United States citizens who are detained under the authority of the United States."[112] In addition, the Bureau of Prisons (BOP) is required to collect a DNA sample from each federal prisoner who is, or has been, convicted of a felony, a sexual abuse crime under chapter 109A of title 18 of the U.S. Code, a crime of violence,[113] or any attempt or conspiracy to commit any of these crimes.[114] Federal probation offices responsible for supervising individuals on probation, parole, or supervised release are required to collect DNA samples from individuals who are, or have been, convicted of any of the crimes outlined above.[115] Collected samples are required to be submitted to the FBI for analysis and their resulting DNA profiles are included in the NDIS.[116]

Current law contains similar provisions regarding the collection of DNA samples from District of Columbia offenders. BOP is required to collect a DNA sample from each prisoner who is, or has been, convicted of a qualifying District of Columbia offense.[117] In addition, the Court Services and Offender Supervision Agency for the District of Columbia is required to collect DNA samples from individuals on probation, parole, or supervised release, who are, or have been, convicted of any qualifying District of Columbia offense.[118] The government of the District of Columbia may determine which offenses under the District of Columbia Code are considered qualifying offenses for the purposes of supplying a DNA sample.[119] Collected samples must be submitted to the FBI for analysis and their resulting DNA profiles are included in the NDIS.[120]

Under current law,[121] the DOD is required to collect DNA samples from each member of the Armed Forces who is, or has been, convicted of an offense under the Uniform Code of Military Justice for which a sentence of confinement of more than one year can be imposed, or of any other offense under the Uniform Code of Military Justice that is comparable to the offenses for which a DNA sample can be collected from a federal offender (see above).[122] DOD is required to conduct an analysis of the collected sample and submit the results to the FBI for inclusion in the NDIS.[123]

Post-conviction DNA Testing

The Justice for All Act of 2004 (P.L. 108-405) established procedures for post-conviction DNA testing in federal courts. Under current law,[124] upon a written motion from an individual sentenced for a federal offense (hereinafter, "applicant"), the court must order DNA testing of evidence if all of the following apply:

- The applicant asserts, under penalty of perjury, that the applicant is actually innocent of the federal crime for which the applicant was sentenced, or another federal or state offense, if (1) "the evidence was entered during a federal death sentence hearing and exoneration for the offense would entitle the applicant to a reduced sentence or a new sentencing hearing"; or (2) "in the case of a [s]tate offense, the applicant demonstrates that there is no adequate remedy under [s]tate law to permit DNA testing of the ... evidence ... and, to the extent available, the applicant has exhausted all remedies available under [s]tate law for requesting DNA testing of ... evidence."
- The specified evidence to be tested was secured in relation to the investigation or prosecution of the federal or state crime for which the applicant claims to be innocent.

- The evidence to be tested (1) "was not previously subjected to DNA testing, and the applicant did not knowingly and voluntarily waive the right to request DNA testing of the evidence in a court proceeding after the date of enactment of the [Justice for All Act of 2004 (October 30, 2004)] or [did not] knowingly fail to request DNA testing of the evidence in a prior motion for post-conviction DNA testing"; or (2) "was previously subjected to DNA testing and the applicant requests DNA testing using a new method or technology that is substantially more probative that prior testing."
- The evidence to be tested "is in the possession of the [g]overnment and has been subject to a chain of custody and retained under conditions sufficient to ensure that such evidence has not been substituted, contaminated, tampered with, replaced, or altered in any respect" that would affect the DNA testing.
- The proposed DNA testing is "reasonable in scope, uses scientifically sound methods, and is consistent with accepted forensic practices."
- The applicant "identifies a theory of defense that is not inconsistent with an affirmative defense presented at trial and would establish the actual innocence of the applicant."
- If the applicant was "convicted following a trial, the identity of the perpetrator was at issue in the trial."
- The proposed DNA testing may produce new material evidence that would support the affirmative defense theory presented at trial and raise a reasonable probability that the applicant did not commit the crime.
- The applicant certifies that he or she will provide a DNA sample for comparison purposes.
- The motion is made in a timely fashion.[125]

If the court orders DNA testing, the testing is carried out by the FBI.[126] However, the court can order DNA testing to be conducted by another "qualified laboratory if the court makes all necessary orders to ensure the integrity of the ... evidence and the reliability of the testing process and results."[127] The cost of any DNA testing is borne by the applicant, unless the applicant is indigent; in that case, the cost of the DNA testing is borne by the government.[128]

Test results relating to the DNA sample provided by the applicant are to be included in the NDIS.[129] If the test results ordered by the court are "inconclusive or show that the applicant was the source of the tested evidence, the applicant's DNA profile may be retained in the NDIS."[130] Moreover, if the test results show that the applicant was not the source of the tested evidence, and a comparison of the applicant's DNA profile with other forensic profiles in the NDIS result in a match, DOJ is to contact the appropriate agency and preserve the applicant's DNA sample.[131]

However, if the test results exclude the applicant as the source of the tested evidence, and a comparison between the applicant's DNA profile and forensic profiles in the NDIS does not result in a match, DOJ must destroy the applicant's DNA sample and ensure that the applicant's DNA profile is not stored in the NDIS if there is no other legal authority to retain the profile in the NDIS.[132]

If the results of the DNA test are inconclusive, the court can order further testing, if appropriate, or it can deny the applicant relief.[133] If the results of the DNA test demonstrate that the applicant was the source of the evidence tested, the applicant is denied relief, and on a motion of the government, the court can determine whether the applicant's claim of actual innocence was false. If the court finds the claim was false, it can

- hold the applicant in contempt of court;
- assess against the applicant any cost of DNA testing;
- forward the findings to BOP, who may wholly, or in part, deny the applicant's good conduct time;[134]
- if the applicant is eligible for parole, forward the finding to the U.S. Parole Commission so the commission can deny parole on the basis of the finding; or
- if the test results relate to a state offense, forward the findings to the appropriate state official.[135]

Under current law, if the applicant is convicted for making false assertions relating to post-conviction DNA testing, the applicant is to be sentenced to no less than three years imprisonment, to run consecutively with any other term of imprisonment the applicant is serving.[136]

If the results of the DNA testing demonstrate that the applicant was not the source of the tested evidence presented as a part of the case against the applicant, the applicant can file a motion for a new trial or resentencing, as appropriate, notwithstanding any law that would bar the motion as untimely.[137] Under current law, the applicant would be granted a new trial or resentencing, if the DNA results, when considered with all other evidence in the case (regardless of whether such evidence was introduced at trial), establish by compelling evidence that a new trial would result in an acquittal of the federal offense the applicant is currently sentenced for, or in the case of resentencing, if evidence of a federal or state offense was admitted during a federal death sentencing hearing and exoneration for the offense would entitle the applicant to a reduced sentence or a new sentencing hearing.[138]

Preservation of Biological Evidence

The Justice for All Act of 2004 (P.L. 108-405), among other things, established standards for the preservation of biological evidence by the government. Under current law,[139] the federal government is required to preserve biological evidence[140] that was secured in the investigation or prosecution of a federal offense, if a defendant was imprisoned for the offense, unless[141]

- "the court denied a request or motion for DNA testing [of the evidence] and no appeal is pending";
- the defendant "knowingly and voluntarily waived the right to request DNA testing [of the evidence] in a court proceeding conducted after the date of enactment of the [Justice for All Act of 2004 (October 30, 2004)]";
- "after a conviction becomes final and the defendant has exhausted all opportunities for direct review of the conviction, the defendant is notified that the evidence may be destroyed and the defendant does not file a motion [for post-conviction DNA testing] within 180 days of receipt of notice";
- "the evidence must be returned to its rightful owner, or it is of such size, bulk, or physical character as to render retention impracticable and the [g]overnment takes reasonable measures to remove and preserve portions of the evidence sufficient to permit future DNA testing"; or
- the evidence has been the subject of post-conviction DNA testing (see above) and the results of the testing demonstrate that the defendant was the source of the evidence.

Grants for DNA-Related Programs

Several grant programs provide assistance to state and local governments for forensic sciences. A bulk of the programs focus on providing state and local governments with funding to reduce the backlog of forensic and convicted offender samples waiting to be processed and entered into the NDIS. However, some grant programs provide funding for other purposes, such as offsetting the cost of providing post-conviction DNA testing. This section of the report provides a brief overview of grants for forensic sciences.

Debbie Smith DNA Backlog Grant Program

The Debbie Smith DNA Backlog Grant Program (hereinafter, "Debbie Smith grants") provides grants to state and local governments for five major purposes: (1) conducting analyses of DNA samples collected under applicable legal authority for inclusion in the NDIS, (2) conducting analyses of forensic DNA samples for inclusion in the NDIS, (3) increasing the capacity of state and local laboratories to carry out DNA analyses, (4) collecting DNA samples from people required to submit them and forensic samples from crimes, and (5) ensuring that analyses of forensic DNA samples are carried out in a timely manner. The Katie Sepich Enhanced DNA Collection Act of 2012 (P.L. 112-253) amended the Debbie Smith program to set aside up to $10 million of the amount appropriated for Debbie Smith grants for FY2013-FY2015 to assist states with the costs associated with collecting DNA samples from arrestees (assuming there is statutory authority in the state to collect DNA sample from people arrested for certain offenses). The Sexual Assault Forensic Evidence Reporting Act of 2013 (the SAFER Act of 2013, Title X of P.L. 113-4) added two new purposes for which Debbie Smith grants can be used: to conduct an audit of the samples of sexual assault evidence in the possession of a state or unit of local government that are awaiting testing and to ensure that the collection and processing of DNA evidence by law enforcement and to ensure the collection and processing of DNA evidence is carried out in a timely manner and in accordance with the protocols and practices the FBI is required to develop under the act.

The Attorney General is required to award funds using a formula. The formula distributes funds amongst state and local governments to maximize the effective utilization of DNA technology to solve crimes and protect public safety. The formula must also allocate funding amongst state and local governments to reduce backlogs by considering the number of offender and forensic samples awaiting DNA analysis in the jurisdiction along with the population and number of violent crimes in the jurisdiction. Current law requires DOJ to award not less than 0.5% of the total amount appropriated each fiscal year to each state and the District of Columbia. The territories are to receive 0.125% of the total appropriation.

Agencies receiving a grant under the program are required to certify that DNA analyses are conducted in laboratories that satisfy the FBI's QAS and are operated either by a state or local government or by a private laboratory under contract with the state or local government. Grants for conducting analyses of DNA samples collected under applicable legal authority for inclusion in the NDIS, conducting analyses of forensic casework for inclusion in the NDIS, and ensuring that analyses of forensic DNA samples are carried out in a timely manner can be made in the form of a contract or voucher for laboratory services that can be redeemed by nonprofit or for-profit laboratories that satisfy the QAS and have been approved by the Attorney General.

State and local governments receiving funding under the program are required to submit a report to DOJ with a summary of the activities carried out under the grant and an assessment of whether such activities are meeting the needs identified in the grant application, as well as other information the Attorney General may require. DOJ may award not more than 1% of grant funding each fiscal year to states, units of local government, and nonprofit professional organizations of persons actively involved in forensic science and nationally recognized within the forensic science community to help offset the cost of accrediting and auditing laboratories.

The SAFER Act of 2013 established a series of conditions for states or units of local government receiving a grant under the Debbie Smith program for the purposes of conducting an audit of sexual assault evidence. The act, among other things, requires states and local governments receiving grants for this purpose to (1) submit a plan for performing an audit of samples, (2) provide an estimate of the number of samples, (3) complete the audit within one year of receiving the grant, and (4) submit a report to DOJ every 60 days for at least one year after the audit is completed that provides data on the number of samples in the state's or unit of local government's possession along with data on new sexual assault evidence the state or local government receives and how those samples are being processed.

The SAFER Act of 2013 also requires the FBI, in consultation with federal, state, and local law enforcement agencies, to develop protocols and practices for the accurate, timely, and effective collection and processing of

DNA evidence, including protocols and practices specific to sexual assault cases. The protocols and practices are required to address (1) what evidence should be collected by law enforcement and forwarded for testing and the order in which that evidence should be tested, (2) a reasonable period of time for evidence to be forwarded to a laboratory for testing, (3) a reasonable period of time in which each stage of laboratory testing should be conducted, (4) a system to encourage communication between actors in the criminal justice system (e.g., law enforcement, courts, and laboratory personnel and crime victims) about the status of evidence testing, and (5) standards for audits of sexual assault evidence in the possession of state and local governments.

Debbie Smith grants were originally authorized under the Justice for All Act of 2004 (P.L. 108- 405). This law amended the DNA Backlog Elimination Act of 2000,[142] authorizing appropriations of $151.0 million for each of FY2004-FY2009.[143] The program was reauthorized under the Debbie Smith Reauthorization Act of 2008 (P.L. 110-360), which includes authorized appropriations of $151.0 million for FY2009-FY2014. A funding history for this program since FY2006 is provided in **Table 2**.

Kirk Bloodsworth Post-Conviction DNA Testing Grant Program

The Kirk Bloodsworth DNA Post-conviction DNA Testing Grant program was authorized by the Justice for All Act of 2004 (P.L. 108-405). The act authorized the Attorney General to make grants to states to help defray the costs of post-conviction DNA testing programs. The act authorized appropriations of $5.0 million for FY2005-FY2009. A funding history for this program since FY2006 is provided in **Table 2**.

Sexual Assault Forensic Exam Program Grants

The Sexual Assault Forensic Exam Program Grants were authorized under the Justice for All Act of 2004 (P.L. 108-405). The program provides grants for training, technical assistance, education, equipment, and information relating to the identification, collection, preservation, analysis, and use of DNA samples and evidence by medical personnel and those treating victims of sexual assault. Under the program, entities eligible to receive grants include states, units of local government, and sexual assault examination programs. The act authorized appropriations of $30.0 million for each of FY2005-

FY2009. P.L. 110-360 extended the same authorized amount through FY2014. A funding history for this program since FY2006 is provided in **Table 2**.

DNA Research and Development Grants

The Justice for All Act of 2004 authorized grants for research and development for improving forensic DNA technology, including increasing the accuracy and efficiency of DNA analysis, decreasing the time and expense of conducting DNA analysis, and increasing its portability. In addition, the law authorized grants for demonstration projects to evaluate the use of DNA technology in conjunction with other forensic analyses. The act authorized funding of $15.0 million for each of FY2005-FY2009. This program has not received any appropriations since FY2006.

DNA Training and Education for Law Enforcement, Correctional Personnel, and Court Officers

Under this program, the Attorney General is required to make grants to provide training, technical assistance, education, and information regarding the identification, collection, preservation, analysis, and use of DNA samples and evidence by law enforcement personnel, court officers, forensic science professionals, and corrections personnel. The program was originally authorized under the Justice for All Act of 2004 (P.L. 108-405), which authorized $12.5 million for each of FY2005-FY2009. P.L. 110-360 extended the same authorized amount through FY2014. This program has not received any appropriations since FY2006.

Appropriations for DNA-Related Grant Programs

Since FY2006, Congress has appropriated over $100 million each fiscal year for DNA analysis and other forensic programs and activities. As shown in **Table 2**, most funding each fiscal year was dedicated to reducing DNA backlogs, enhancing crime laboratory capacity, and other activities related to DNA analysis.

Table 2. Appropriations for Forensic Science Grant Programs Appropriations in millions of dollars

	FY2006	FY2007	FY2008	FY2009	FY2010	FY2011	FY2012	FY2013[a]	FY2014
DNA-Related and Forensic Programs and Activities	107.1	112.1	152.3	156.0	161.0	133.4	125.0	116.2	125.0
DNA Analysis, Capacity Enhancement, and Debbie Smith Grants	*(103.2)*	*(108.2)*	*(147.4)*	*(151.0)*	*(151.0)*	*(125.1)*	*(117.0)*	*(108.8*[b]*)*	*(117.0*[b]*)*
Kirk Bloodsworth Post-conviction DNA Testing	*(3.9)*	*(3.9)*	*(4.9)*	*(5.0)*	*(5.0)*	*(4.1)*	*(4.0)*	*(3.7)*	*(4.0)*
Sexual Assault Forensic Exam		—	—	—	*(5.0)*	*(4.1)*	*(4.0)*	*(3.7)*	*(4.0)*

Source: FY2006-enacted appropriations are taken from OJP's FY2008 congressional budget submission; FY2007-enacted appropriations are taken from OJP's FY2009 congressional budget submission; FY2008-enacted appropriations are taken from OJP's FY2010 congressional budget submission; and FY2009- and FY2010-enacted appropriations are taken from OJP's FY2011 congressional budget submission; FY2011-enacted appropriations are based on a CRS analysis of the text of P.L. 112-10; FY2012-enacted appropriations are taken from H.Rept. 112-284; FY2013 appropriation provided by the U.S. Department of Justice; FY2014-enacted amounts were taken from the joint explanatory statement to accompany P.L. 113-76, printed in the January 15, 2014, *Congressional Record* (pp. H507-H532).

Notes: Amounts under the DNA-Related and Forensic Programs and Activities might not sum to total due to rounding.

[a] The FY2013 enacted amount includes a 1.877% rescission per section 3001 of P.L. 113-6 and a 0.2% rescission ordered by the Office of Management and Budget per section 3004 of P.L. 113-6. The FY2013 enacted amount also includes the amount sequestered per the Budget Control Act of 2011(P.L. 112-25).

[b] Up to 4% of the funding for DNA analysis can be used for the purposes described under the DNA Training and Education for Law Enforcement, Correctional Personnel, and Court Officers program.

In FY2006 and FY2007, Congress gave the Administration discretion in how to award appropriated funding for DNA-related activities. The report to accompany the FY2006 Science, State, Justice, Commerce, and Related Agencies Appropriations Act (P.L. 109-108) stated that the appropriation was for a "capacity enhancement program including eliminating casework backlogs, eliminating offender backlogs, strengthening crime lab capacity, training of the criminal justice community and identifying missing persons."[144] Starting in FY2008, Congress continued to appropriate funding for DNA analysis and capacity enhancement, *including* Debbie Smith grants.[145] The language in the FY2008-FY2014 appropriations bills did not require DOJ to use *all* of the funding for DNA analysis and capacity enhancement for Debbie Smith grants, rather, it just had to award a portion of the funding for the programs. As such, DOJ has awarded funding it received for DNA analysis and capacity enhancement under a variety of programs, including Forensic DNA Backlog Reduction, Convicted Offender DNA Backlog Reduction, Forensic Science Training Development and Delivery, Forensic DNA Unit Efficiency Improvement, Solving Cold Cases with DNA Evidence, DNA to Identify Missing Persons, and DNA Research and Development.[146]

SELECTED ISSUES FOR CONGRESS

In the 1990s and the early part of the last decade, most of the debate about the use of DNA in criminal justice centered on the scope of DNA databases, reducing the backlog of DNA casework, and providing access to post-conviction DNA testing. Most of this debate faded with the enactment of the Violence Against Women and Department of Justice Reauthorization Act of 2005 (P.L. 109-162), which expanded federal collection statutes to include anyone arrested or detained under the authority of the United States. The act also expanded the scope of the NDIS to include DNA profiles of individuals arrested for state crimes. However, concerns about the backlog of DNA casework have persisted. In addition, new issues related to the use of DNA in criminal justice have emerged, including whether (1) DNA databases should be used to conduct familial searches, (2) sexual assault evidence collections kits should be standardized, and (3) there should be national accreditation standard for forensic laboratories. Each of these issues are discussed in more detail below.

The NDIS and Familial Searching

The debate over familial searching is framed by the question of how to balance the desire of law enforcement agencies to use all available tools for solving crimes against the privacy of individuals who might fall under suspicion because they happen to be related to someone convicted, or in some cases arrested, for a crime. The success of familial searching depends on a close relationship between someone with a profile in the database and the unknown perpetrator.[147] Proponents of familial searching cite research that indicates children of parents who have been convicted of a crime are more likely themselves to be convicted of a crime. Further, siblings who have been convicted are more likely to have other siblings who have been convicted.[148] Proponents also cite data from the Bureau of Justice Statistics (BJS) indicating that 46% of jail inmates reported that they had at least one close relative who had been incarcerated.[149] However, opponents of familial searching challenge its empirical basis. They stress that if offenders are more likely to have *convicted* relatives then their relatives' profiles would already be in the database and there would be no need to expand database searches to include non-convicted relatives.[150] Also, conviction data might not be a perfect indicator of criminal propensity. Biases in the criminal justice system, both racial and geographical, might lead certain groups of people, namely racial and ethnic minorities living in urban centers, to be arrested and convicted more than others with a similar rate of criminality. It could be possible that a law-abiding individual is more likely than a convicted offender to have a convicted relative.[151] On the other hand, many people commit crimes for which they are never arrested or convicted, so it is also possible that convicted offenders have relatives who have committed crimes for which there is no official record.

One of the primary privacy concerns regarding the use of familial searching is that it will put innocent people under "genetic surveillance" because they are related to someone whose profile is in a DNA database.[152] Proponents of familial searching argue that while an offender's family could be questioned by law enforcement as a result of a partial match, they could also come under the scrutiny of law enforcement during the course of an investigation that did not use familial searching.[153] For instance, an eyewitness viewing a lineup may indicate that one face bears a strong resemblance to—but is not actually—the perpetrator; at this point law enforcement might turn attention to a suspect's brother or other relatives. Relatives could also come under suspicion because the investigation turned up evidence of their involvement. Proponents also argue that familial searching might actually *exclude* relatives as the potential perpetrator.[154] Opponents counter that familial searching does not search the entire pool of suspects. Rather, it only subjects relatives of convicted offenders to potential law enforcement scrutiny; relatives of individuals who have not been convicted of, or arrested for, a crime are not at risk of becoming the subject of an investigation through familial searching.[155] Also, some opponents assert, if society has an interest in identifying perpetrators and exonerating the innocent by using a method that would subject non-convicted individuals to law enforcement scrutiny, then the most equitable and optimal mean to achieve this goal is universal DNA collection so that everyone, not just those who are related to someone with a profile in a DNA database, can share in the burdens and benefits of DNA databases.[156]

It has been estimated that using familial searching could increase the cold hit rate (i.e., a match in the database between an offender or arrestee profile and a forensic profile from a case where there is no suspect) in the United States from 10% to 14%.[157] However, opponents argue that familial searching would strain law enforcement's resources because they will have to investigate multiple leads, and in some cases all of the leads might be false-positives. Proponents counter this claim by noting that procedures could be put in place to reduce the number of leads to only the most promising ones. For example, laboratories could use kinship analysis to calculate the probability that a known offender DNA profile in the databases is related to the individual who left a DNA sample at the crime scene.[158] Y-chromosome analysis could, for instance, help determine whether a known offender in the database and the unknown suspect who left a DNA sample at a crime scene are related through male lineage and analysis of mitochondrial DNA (mtDNA) could help determine whether two people are related through maternal lineage.[159] While kinship analysis would make familial searching more efficient, DNA databases are currently not equipped to conduct them.[160] In addition, Y-chromosome and mitochondrial DNA analysis would require additional testing of both the known offender and the forensic samples.

Opponents argue that familial searching would exacerbate existing racial and ethnic disparities in the criminal justice system. African Americans and Hispanics, compared to whites, are disproportionately arrested and convicted, and since the NDIS is comprised of samples collected from individuals arrested and convicted for qualifying offenses, minorities are more likely to have profiles in the NDIS.[161] Disparities in the racial/ethnic compositions of profiles in the NDIS could mean that minority groups would be disproportionately investigated as a result of familial searches.[162] It was estimated that using the NDIS for familial searching could mean that approximately 17% of the African American population in the United States would be "findable" through the database, compared to approximately 4% of the white population (which includes non-African American Hispanics).[163] Disparities in who is investigated as a result of familial searching could also compound existing disparities in the criminal justice system, assuming that more investigations would result in more arrests and convictions.[164] While proponents of familial searching acknowledge that minority groups are more likely to become suspects in investigations resulting from familial searching, they argue that minority groups might benefit from the policy because crime is disproportionately intraracial, meaning that victims of crimes are more likely to be from minority groups.[165] Therefore, minority groups may be more likely to benefit from crimes being solved through familial searching.[166] Proponents have also argued that even if an investigative technique like familial searching does have a disproportionate effect on a specific group, it is not grounds to forgo the technique if it will solve crimes.[167]

Another privacy concern about the use of familial testing is that it could disrupt families. Specifically, opponents of familial searching have voiced concerns that someone might learn that (1) a relative had an unknown criminal history, (2) there is an existing unknown biological relationship between two people, or (3) there is no biological relationship between two people who assume they are related. However, the threat that familial searching poses to families appears to be proportional to how thorough and discreet law enforcement is in investigating leads generated by the search. Proponents argue that family secrets would only be exposed if law enforcement reveals how and why the suspect became a target of the investigation.[168] Since partial matches only suggest that an unknown perpetrator and a known offender might be related, it is unlikely that law enforcement would be able to obtain a warrant to compel the individual to provide a DNA sample.[169] Hence, law enforcement would need to investigate the lead further and develop corroborating evidence that the relative might be the unknown perpetrator. As such, law enforcement would most likely not have to share with the subject of the investigation that the lead was generated through a familial search. In cases where a DNA sample is collected from a suspect, law enforcement should be able to test it against the forensic sample to determine if the suspect committed the crime. They would not have to let the suspect know that they are not related to the person whose profile generated the lead.[170] In addition, law enforcement can legally collect and analyze DNA samples from items the suspect discarded in an area where the suspect had no expectation of privacy (for example, saliva on a soda can the suspect threw away), which would allow law enforcement to surreptitiously exclude a suspect as the possible offender.[171] Proponents have noted that law enforcement could also uncover personal information about a suspect or a suspect's family during the course of an investigation that involved alternative types of surveillance or searches.[172] Yet, despite measures taken by law enforcement to not expose any family secrets, when law enforcement investigates biological relationships, there is the possibility that previously unknown relationships might be revealed.[173]

As outlined above, Congress has delineated the scope of the NDIS in law, but the law is silent as to how the NDIS can be used to make matches. In the conference report for the Commerce, Justice, Science, and Related Agencies Act, 2011 (P.L. 112-55), Congress encouraged the FBI to "undertake activities to facilitate familial DNA searches of the [NDIS] and ... consider the establishment of procedures allowing familial searches only for serious violent and sexual crimes where other investigative leads have been exhausted."[174] Congress also specified that the procedures "should provide appropriate protections for the privacy rights" of individuals with a profile in the NDIS.[175] While Congress has encouraged the FBI to open up the NDIS for familial searching, there are a couple of issues Congress might consider related to this. First, if a potential familial match is made using the NDIS, should law enforcement be required to conduct additional testing before the lead is investigated further (such as Y-chromosome and mtDNA testing of both the forensic and offender DNA samples or searching public records to determine if the offender and the suspect are related)? Second, should there be additional funding for the FBI or the Office of Justice Programs to provide training to law enforcement on how to investigate leads resulting from familial matching so as to decrease any risk of accidently revealing family secrets?

Reducing the Backlog

If Congress chooses to consider legislation to reduce the size of the DNA backlog, two options it might consider are increasing the capacity of state and local laboratories to conduct DNA analyses and facilitating partnerships between public and private laboratories.

Enhancing the Capacity of State and Local Laboratories

As described above, Debbie Smith grants can be used by state and local laboratories to reduce offender and forensic casework backlogs and enhance their capacity to conduct DNA analyses. This program represents the primary mechanism by which Congress has promoted efforts to reduce the DNA backlog. A study of DNA backlogs in 2007 found that there is a need for Debbie Smith grants. Of the laboratories responding to the survey, 83% replied that they would expect an increase in forensic casework backlogs if they did not receive Debbie Smith grants.[176] Moreover, nearly 90% of laboratories responded that state and local funding would not be sufficient if they did not receive federal support.[177] The study also found that while laboratories are better prepared to process offender and arrestee samples, they still rely on federal funding to conduct these analyses. Nearly 61% of responding laboratories reported that they would expect an increase in offender and arrestee sample backlogs if they no longer received Debbie Smith grants.[178] However, it is possible that respondents to the survey overstated the need for federal support out of fear that federal funding for DNA backlogs could be curtailed or eliminated if there was not a large demand for it.

Data from the BJS's 2009 Census of Publicly Funded Forensic Crime Laboratories indicates that backlogs of DNA evidence persist. There was a 12% increase in the number of backlogged (defined as a pending request for analysis that had not been completed in at least 30 days) forensic casework samples between the end of 2008 (355,300) and the end of 2009 (398,900).[179] There was a 4% decrease in convicted offender/arrestee samples over this same time period, but at the end of 2009 there were still 494,400 convicted offender/arrestee samples awaiting analysis.[180] Forensic crime labs also reported that at the end of 2009 there was a backlog of 19,000 requests to process sexual assault evidence kits, but this was down from a backlog of 21,000 kits at the end of 2008.[181]

Congress may choose to consider the role the federal government should play in reducing state DNA backlogs. Large backlogs can delay the resolution of criminal investigations, and Congress might have an interest in ensuring that as many criminals as possible are apprehended. As discussed above, it appears that laboratories rely on federal funding to help reduce backlogs, especially forensic casework backlogs. In addition, even though Congress has appropriated approximately $1.062 billion for backlog reduction and laboratory capacity enhancement programs since FY2006 (see **Table 2**), data show that backlogs of offender and forensic casework are persistent. States have expanded the pool of people who are required to submit DNA samples, and law enforcement agencies have started to collect biological evidence in more cases. But the increasing demand for DNA analysis has not been met with increased capacity to conduct the analyses. One policy option policy makers could consider is increasing authorized appropriations for the Debbie Smith grants over the current $151 million per fiscal year. While providing additional funding to states for backlog reduction could allow them to hire more analysts to work on reducing the backlog, it is likely that it would take some time to bring the backlog down from current levels. It can take up to one year to recruit, interview, and hire a new analyst; and it can take another year or two until the analyst is fully trained.[182] In addition, the workloads of more experienced analysts might actually decrease when new analysts are hired because the more experienced analysts will have to train and review the work of the new analysts.[183] Congress might also consider whether to allow Debbie Smith grants to be used for capital investments, such as new construction to expand crime laboratories. Hiring additional staff might ultimately help reduce DNA backlogs, but there could be a limit on the number of staff crime laboratories can hire given space constraints.

However, while Congress might have an interest in helping states resolve their backlogs of DNA samples, there might be some concern that by relying on federal funding to support the operations of state and local laboratories, state and local administrators would be unaware of laboratories' true funding needs, which would prevent them from seeking permanent funding solutions. It could be argued that states have contributed to the backlog problem by expanding DNA collection statutes before increasing their capacity to process the samples they were already collecting. DNA backlogs are not a static phenomenon; they will continue to increase or decrease depending on the demand for DNA analysis and the ability of crime laboratories to conduct the requested analyses. Therefore, the backlog cannot simply be eliminated by providing enough funding to state and local crime laboratories to analyze the number of samples in their backlog for any given point in time; the backlog will only be eliminated when capacity is adequate to meet demand. This means that unless state and local governments make the required investment in crime laboratory capacity, they will likely need continued federal funding to manage backlogs. Congress could consider phasing-out funding for the program to provide states with an incentive to invest in increasing and maintaining their capacity to conduct DNA analyses. Congress could also consider amending the authorizing legislation Debbie Smith grants to make it a matching grant program. Another option may be limiting the number of years states could receive funding under the program so that states would have to consider revenue streams for permanently funding crime laboratories.

Congress might consider whether to modify the Debbie Smith grant program so that a greater proportion of the funding goes to reducing the forensic casework backlog. NIJ reports that demand for grants to assist with reducing the backlog of convicted offender and arrestee samples peaked in FY2007 and has decreased in subsequent fiscal years.[184] As mentioned, currently not less than 40% of the amount appropriated for the program is to be awarded for grants to conduct analyses of forensic DNA samples for inclusion in the NDIS. Given that laboratories appear to be better prepared to process offender and arrestee samples than they are to process forensic casework samples, Congress might consider amending the authorizing statute for Debbie Smith grants so that DOJ is required to award a greater proportion of annual funding for the program to laboratories for reducing the backlog of forensic casework.

Congress could also consider providing additional funding to state and local laboratories for the purchase or development and testing of new technology that will help automate more of the DNA analysis process. Automating some of the more labor-intensive parts of DNA analysis, such as DNA extraction or reviewing the results of the analysis, could help laboratories process more samples in a shorter period of time, thereby reducing the backlog. While automation might help reduce backlogs in the long run, it is unlikely that it would have an immediate effect on reducing backlogs. It can take months to implement and validate new equipment, processes, and procedures, and doing so takes personnel away from working on processing current casework.[185]

Another consideration might be whether to provide funding to help state and local law enforcement to either hire additional investigators or offset the cost of paying overtime to current investigators so they can investigate leads generated by DNA database matches. As discussed, law enforcement agencies have identified funding for either additional staffing for cold case units or paying overtime if the agency does not have a cold case unit as a primary need for DNA-related work. However, there could be a concern that state and local governments will come to rely on federal funding for supporting cold case units rather than identifying permanent revenue streams.

Facilitating Partnerships between Public and Private Laboratories

As discussed above, if a public laboratory outsources some casework to a private laboratory, the public laboratory must review the work of the private laboratory before it is uploaded into the NDIS, even though both public and private laboratories have to be accredited and audited in order to conduct DNA analyses that will generate profiles for inclusion in the NDIS. In many instances, public laboratories do not have additional analysts to review work outsourced to private laboratories. Hence, the requirement that public laboratories check the work of DNA profiles generated by private laboratories might discourage public-private partnerships.[186] Also, in cases where laboratories do not have adequate resources, analysts have to review DNA profiles outsourced to private laboratories in addition to their regular casework, meaning that analysts are paid overtime, which makes the cost of outsourcing the sample more expensive. Further, it takes additional time for the work to be reviewed, resulting in a delayed uploading into the NDIS.[187]

One possible issue before Congress is whether to amend federal policy to facilitate partnerships between public and private laboratories. Congress could consider amending current law so that public laboratories do not have to review the work of private laboratories that are in compliance with the QAS. This might facilitate more public-private partnerships since public laboratories would be able to upload DNA profiles into the NDIS without having to review the private laboratory's work. One potential benefit to outsourcing more samples to private laboratories is that private laboratories might be able to analyze samples at a lower cost than public laboratories. In his testimony before the House Subcommittee on Crime, Terrorism, and Homeland Security, Dr. Jeffery Boschwitz noted that the cost of analyzing DNA samples in private laboratories can be up to 50% less than the cost of comparable analyses conducted by public laboratories.[188] Dr. Boschwitz notes that private laboratories can offer lower per case costs because private laboratories can leverage economies of scale and they have invested in research and development to lower costs in order to remain competitive.[189] However, law enforcement agencies or prosecutors would have to pay private laboratory analysts an expert testimony fee to testify in court, a cost they do not have to bear when an analyst from a public laboratory testifies. This could be a significant cost for local law enforcement agencies or prosecutors in light of the Supreme Court's ruling in *Melendez-Diaz v. Massachusetts* that defendants have a Sixth Amendment right to cross-examine an analyst who conducts an analysis of forensic evidence used in the case against the defendant.[190] However, Dr. Boschwitz testified that, in his experience, most defense attorneys do not ask for DNA testing-related testimony.[191] He testified that analysts in his laboratory are asked to testify, on average, in 2% of the cases they analyze, even after the *Melendez-Diaz* decision.[192] Nonetheless, it is not known whether other private laboratories experiences with analysts being called to testify mirror those of Dr. Boschwitz's laboratory or whether trends will change in the future. Partnerships between public and private laboratories could also provide public laboratories with a temporary increase in capacity when there is a unexpected increase in requests for DNA analysis.[193] By outsourcing more work, public laboratories could increase their capacity to a level where they would be able to handle the regular demand for DNA analysis without having to develop a surplus capacity to handle occasional increases in demand. This could promote more efficient public laboratories since they would not need to hire additional staff or purchase additional equipment to prepare for instances where there is increased demand for DNA analysis.

Some advocates of reducing DNA backlogs by having private laboratories conduct more DNA analyses might propose allowing private laboratories to have direct access to CODIS. After all, private laboratories are held to the same standard as public crime laboratories. This proposal raises one of the key questions about any public-private partnership in criminal justice: are some functions of the system inherently governmental? As discussed above, in some states laboratories retain the DNA sample that is used to generate the databased profile. This is done so that samples can be retested to confirm matches made using CODIS and to allow laboratories to retest samples in case of any technological advancements. If private laboratories were allowed direct access to CODIS, it might raise a question about whether it would be prudent for private laboratories to retain DNA samples. Another consideration might be whether involving private laboratories in investigating criminal offenses could decrease the efficiency of the investigation. When a match is made between a forensic and offender profile, there are several additional steps that must take place before charging the suspect with the crime. These steps include, but are not limited to,

- obtaining the personal identification of the subject whose DNA profile matches the forensic profile,
- verifying whether the person is the correct sex and in the appropriate age range to be the perpetrator,
- confirming that the suspect was not in custody at the time of the offense and had access to the crime scene when the offense occurred,
- corroborating the match between the offender and forensic profiles after collecting a new sample from the suspect, and
- determining if other non-DNA evidence supports or refutes that the person could be a viable suspect.[194]

While private laboratories would be able to verify the match between forensic and sample profiles, it is likely that law enforcement would have to be involved with the other steps in moving from a cold hit to a criminal charge. The coordination between the private laboratory and law enforcement could be complicated if the private laboratory is in another city or even another state. Policy makers might consider whether cold hits could be investigated more efficiently if the analysis was done "in-house."

There could be some concern that private laboratories might cut corners as a way to increase profit margins, thereby resulting in flawed DNA profiles being included in the NDIS. While this is a valid concern—after all, flawed DNA profiles could mean that a crime goes unsolved or that the wrong person is convicted for the crime—thus far there has not been an evaluation of whether private laboratories are more likely than public laboratories to make mistakes in their analysis. Before deciding on whether to allow public laboratories to forego reviewing DNA profiles generated by private laboratories, or granting private laboratories access to CODIS, Congress could consider requiring an independent evaluation of whether private laboratories that are in compliance with the conditions of the QAS make errors at a different rate than that of public laboratories.

Annual Backlog Data

As discussed, there is a lack of comprehensive annual data on the size of the forensic casework and offender and arrestee sample backlogs. The data collected by NIJ only provide an estimate of the national forensic casework backlog. They do not include a state-by-state breakdown of the backlog, nor do they estimate the nature of the backlog. Having reliable data on the size and nature of the DNA backlog could provide policy makers with information about the efficacy of existing policies, and it could assist policy makers if they choose to consider other policies for reducing the backlog.

Policy makers might consider creating a system to collect annual DNA backlog data. Currently, state and local governments that receive Debbie Smith grants are required to submit an annual report to DOJ that contains a summary of the activities carried out using grant funds and any other information DOJ might require;[195] but state and local governments are not required to submit data on backlogs, unless required by DOJ. If Congress chooses to consider legislation related to this issue, it might consider requiring states to report data on the size of their forensic casework and offender and arrestee (if applicable) sample backlogs as a condition of receiving Debbie Smith grants. Congress could also consider reducing a state's allocation under the Edward Byrne Memorial Justice Assistance Grant (JAG) program (which provides assistance to state and local law enforcement for a variety of purposes) if a state did not submit annual backlog data to DOJ.[196] One advantage of these methods is that it provides a financial incentive for states to report backlog data. However, there might be a concern about making a state ineligible for Debbie Smith grants or reducing a state's allocation under the JAG program since funding under both programs can be used to help reduce DNA backlogs.

Congress could consider requiring BJS to conduct an annual survey of publicly funded crime laboratories to collect data on DNA backlogs. One advantage to this method is that it would not make a state ineligible for funding that could be used for DNA analysis. On the other hand, it would rely on states to voluntarily provide the data. There might be concern on the part of some policy makers that states will not submit backlog data unless there is a reason for them to do so. The concern is not unfounded because response rates to surveys can vary. However, surveys conducted by BJS tend to have high response rates. For example, 97% of laboratories contacted by BJS to participate in the 2009 Survey of Publicly Funded Forensic Crime Laboratories responded to the survey.[197]

If policy makers choose to establish a system for collecting data on DNA backlogs, they might also consider the scope of the data collected. Would states only be required to submit a count of the number of forensic casework samples in their backlog, or would they also be required to provide a breakdown of the different types of forensic casework samples in their backlog, such as the number of sexual assault evidence collection kits? Should states be required to provide data on the amount of time it takes laboratories to complete the analysis of different types of samples? Should states provide data on backlogged DNA samples for the state in total or should states be required to submit data on backlogs at each local lab that provides DNA profiles to the SDIS?

Standardization of Sexual Assault Evidence Collection Kits

As discussed, the contents of a sexual assault evidence collection kit and the protocols governing whether the kit is submitted to a crime laboratory for analysis can vary from jurisdiction to jurisdiction, which could mean that the quantity and quality of evidence collected in a sexual assault case and the probability that the evidence will be analyzed could depend in part on where the sexual assault occurred. Policy makers might consider legislation that would provide for the standardization of the contents of sexual assault evidence kits.

One issue before Congress is whether it wants to make adopting a standardized sexual assault evidence collection kit a condition of receiving Debbie Smith grants. Another option involves reducing a state or local government's allocation under the JAG program if they choose not to use the standardized kit. If Congress chooses to consider such legislation, one question before policy makers might be whether to specify the exact contents of all sexual assault evidence collection kits used in the United States, or whether to establish a minimum standard for kits and allow jurisdictions to add additional elements if they choose. In their national protocol for sexual assault medical examinations, the Office on Violence Against Women (OVW) provided guidelines for the minimum content of sexual assault evidence collection kits. The guidelines state that, at a minimum, sexual assault evidence collection kits should include

- a kit container which has a label with blanks for identifying information and documenting the chain of custody;
- an instruction sheet or checklist to guide examiners in collecting evidence and maintaining the chain of custody;
- forms that facilitate evidence collection and analysis, including the patient's authorization for collection and release of evidence and information for law enforcement, the patient's medical history, and anatomical diagrams; and
- materials for collecting and preserving evidence, according to jurisdictional policy, including the patient's clothing and underwear and foreign material dislodged from clothing; foreign materials on the patient's body (e.g., blood, dried secretions, fibers, loose hairs, vegetation, soil/debris, fingernail scrapings and/or cuttings, matted hair cuttings, material dislodged from mouth using dental floss, and swabs of suspected semen, saliva, and/or areas highlighted by alternate light sources); hair evidence; vaginal/cervical swabs and smears; penile swabs and smears; anal/perianal swabs and smears; oral swabs and smears; body swabs; and a sample of the patient's DNA for comparison purposes.[198]

OVW noted it could be beneficial to develop a standardized kit for use across the country, but that "[f]urther analysis is needed to assess the benefits and disadvantages of such a kit and the feasibility of development and implementation. Some challenges could include building consensus across communities regarding best practices and obtaining buy-in from involved agencies."[199] CRS did not find any evaluations of the benefits and disadvantages of a standardized sexual assault evidence collection kit and the feasibility of its development and implementation. Before requiring states and local governments to adopt a standardized sexual assault evidence collection kit as a condition of receiving funding under certain programs, Congress could consider requiring OVW or another DOJ agency to evaluate the feasibility of a standardized sexual assault evidence collection kit.

Federal Accreditation Standards

One issue policy makers might consider is whether there is a need for national accreditation standards for forensic laboratories. Currently, nine states require forensic science laboratories in the state to be accredited.[200] However, even with the lack of state law requiring laboratories to be accredited, most publicly funded laboratories are still seeking and maintaining accreditation. BJS, in their 2009 census of publicly funded crime laboratories, found that 83% of crime laboratories were accredited.[201] In addition, as discussed above, all CODIS laboratories must be accredited and audited annually and analysts at these laboratories are required to undergo semiannual proficiency testing; however, these standards only apply to DNA analysis functions and not to any other forensics analyses the crime laboratory might conduct (e.g., ballistics testing, fingerprint analysis, or toxicology). While national accreditation standards would ensure that all laboratories are held to the same standard and they might help prevent embarrassing incidents where faulty procedures or downright deception has resulted in erroneous DNA analyses, accreditation can only ensure that procedures and practices are in place that would reduce the likelihood of flawed results; it cannot eliminate them. Even if a laboratory is accredited, it is still possible that human error or malignant intentions would mean that the results of some DNA analyses are incorrect. It is also possible that a private accrediting organization like ACSLD/LAB would be able to amend its accreditation standards faster to reflect changes in technology or practice than a federal board could, especially one that is charged with overseeing accreditation standards for all forensic crime laboratories.

All laboratories that receive Debbie Smith grants are required to adhere to the FBI's QAS, which requires the laboratories to be audited annually to ensure that they adhere to the QAS and requires analysts to undergo semiannual proficiency testing. Also, in order to receive funding under the Paul Coverdell Forensic Sciences Improvement Grant program, any forensic science laboratory system, medical examiner's office, or coroner's office (including any laboratory operated by a unit of local government) receiving grant funding uses generally accepted laboratory practices and procedures established by accrediting organizations or appropriate certifying bodies. It appears that current law would prohibit unaccredited laboratories from receiving grants under most currently funded grant programs. However, laboratories would not be prohibited from receiving funding under *all* grant programs (e.g., the Edward Byrne Memorial Justice Assistance Grant program) under which they could possibly receive support. Instead of creating a new office to promulgate and enforce national accreditation standards, Congress could consider amending current law to require state and local governments to certify that any funding they receive under any federal grant program for a forensic science laboratory has received and maintained accreditation from a nonprofit professional organization of persons actively involved in forensic science that is nationally recognized within the forensic science community.

End Notes

[1] See CRS Report RL30717, *DNA Identification: Applications and Issues*, by Eric A. Fischer.

[2] This report does not include a discussion of the use of DNA to identify missing persons and unidentified human remains, nor does it include an overview of grant programs to state and local governments for developing DNA profiles from samples from missing persons, close relatives of missing persons, or unidentified human remains. For more on this issue, see CRS Report RL34616, *Missing Adults: Background, Federal Programs, and Issues for Congress*, by Adrienne L. Fernandes-Alcantara.

[3] Statement of Dwight E. Adams, Deputy Assistant Director, Laboratory Division, Federal Bureau of Investigation, in U.S. Congress, House of Representatives, Government Reform Committee, Subcommittee on Government Efficiency, Financial Management and Intergovernmental Relations, *How Effective are State and Federal Agencies Working Together to Implement the Use of New DNA Technologies*?, hearing, 107th Cong., 1st sess., March 29, 2004, pp. 53-54, at http://www.fbi.gov/congress

[4] John M. Butler, *Fundamentals of Forensic DNA Typing* (Burlington, MA: Academic Press, 2010), p. 265 (hereinafter, *Fundamentals of Forensic DNA Typing*).

[5] Ibid.

[6] U.S. Department of Justice, Federal Bureau of Investigation, *Frequently Asked Questions (FAQs) on the CODIS Program and the National DNA Index System*, _http://www.fbi.gov/about-us/lab/biometric-analysis/codis/codis-andndis-fact-sheet, hereinafter "CODIS FAQs."

[7] U.S. Department of Justice, Federal Bureau of Investigation, *CODIS—NDIS Statistics*, http://www.fbi.gov/about-us/ lab/codis/ndis-statistics.

[8] The National Conference of State Legislatures (NCSL) maintains a searchable database of state DNA laws, including laws related to which convicted offenders are required to submit a sample for inclusion in the state's DNA database and whether, and if so, from whom, collects DNA samples from individuals arrested for certain crimes. The NCSL's database is available online at http://www.ncsl.org/research/civil-and-criminal-justice/dna-laws-database.aspx.

[9] U.S. Department of Justice, Federal Bureau of Investigation, *CODIS—NDIS Statistics*, http://www.fbi.gov/about-us/ lab/codis/ndis-statistics.

[10] CODIS FAQs.

[11] Ibid.

[12] Ibid. If an "offender hit" is obtained, that information typically is used as probable cause to obtain a new DNA sample from that suspect so the match can be confirmed by the crime laboratory before an arrest is made.

[13] Ibid.

[14] CODIS FAQs.

[15] Ibid.

[16] Jules Epstein, "Genetic Surveillance—The *Bogeyman* Response to Familial DNA Investigations," *University of Illinois Journal of Law, Technology and Policy*, vol. 2009, no. 1, (2009), p. 143 (hereinafter, "Epstein, 'Genetic Surveillance'").

[17] Henry T. Greely, Daniel P. Riordan, and Nanibaa' A. Garrison et al., "Family Ties: The Use of DNA Offender Databases to Catch Offenders' Kin," *Journal of Law, Medicine and Ethics*, vol. 34, no. 2 (Summer 2006), p. 250 (hereinafter, "Greely, Riordan, Garrison et al., 'Family Ties'").

[18] Ibid.

[19] *Fundamentals of Forensic DNA Typing*, p. 270.

[20] Ibid., p. 271.

[21] U.S. Department of Justice, Federal Bureau of Investigation, *Quality Assurance Standards for DNA Databasing Laboratories*, Standard 15, http://www.fbi.gov/about-us/lab/biometric-analysis/codis/qas_databaselabs. U.S. Department of Justice, Federal Bureau of Investigation, *Quality Assurance Standards for Forensic DNA Testing Laboratories*, Standard 15, http://www.fbi.gov/about-us/lab/biometric-analysis/codis/qas_testlabs (hereinafter "QAS").

[22] *Fundamentals of Forensic DNA Typing*, p. 271.

[23] Ibid.

[24] Ibid.

[25] U.S. Congress, House Committee on the Judiciary, Subcommittee on Crime, Terrorism, and Homeland Security, *Testimony of Jeffery S. Boschwitz, Ph.D.*, Hearing on "Rape Kit Backlogs: Failing the Test of Providing Justice to Sexual Assault Survivors", 111th Cong., 2nd sess., May 20, 2010, H.Hrg 111-115 (Washington: GPO, 2010), p. 81 (hereinafter, "Testimony of Dr. Boschwitz")

[26] QAS, Standard 17.

[27] CODIS FAQs.

[28] QAS, Standard 17.

[29] Ibid.

[30] *Fundamentals of Forensic DNA Typing*, p. 270.

[31] Ibid., p. 262.

[32] Ibid.

[33] Tania Simoncelli, "Dangerous Excursions: The Case Against Expanding Forensic DNA Databases to Innocent Persons," *Journal of Law, Medicine, and Ethics*, vol. 34, no. 2 (Summer 2006), p. 392 (hereinafter "Simoncelli, 'Dangerous Excursions'").

[34] Simoncelli, "Dangerous Excursions," p. 392.

[35] 42 U.S.C. §14135e(c).

[36] Frederick R. Bieber, "Turning Base Hits into Earned Runs: Improving the Effectiveness of Forensic DNA Data Bank Programs," *Journal of Law, Medicine and Ethics*, vol. 34, no. 2 (Summer 2006), p. 227.

[37] Ibid.

[38] Matthew Gabriel, Cherisse Boland, and Cydne Holt, "Beyond the Cold Hit: Measuring the Impact of the National DNA Data Bank on Public Safety at the City and County Level," *Journal of Law, Medicine and Ethics*, vol. 38, no. 2 (Summer 2010), pp. 396-411.

[39] Ibid., p. 397. "Cold cases" were defined as crimes where the investigation has not generated a named suspect(s) through traditional methods of police investigation (e.g., interviewing witnesses, identification through non-DNA physical evidence left at the crime scene, or tips from confidential informants).

[40] Ibid., p. 398.

[41] Ibid., p. 400.

[42] Ibid.

[43] Edwin Zedlewski and Mary B. Murphy, "DNA Analysis for 'Minor' Crimes: A Major Benefit for Law Enforcement," *NIJ Journal*, vol. 253 (January 2006) (hereinafter, "DNA Analysis for 'Minor' Crimes").

[44] NIJ defines a backlogged case as a case that has not been analyzed within 30 days of being submitted to the laboratory. Mark Nelson, *Making Sense of DNA Backlogs—Myths vs. Reality*, U.S. Department of Justice, Office of Justice Programs, National Institute of Justice, NCJ 323197, Washington, DC, February 2011, p. 3, http://www.ncjrs.gov/pdffiles1/nij/232197.pdf (hereinafter, *Making Sense of DNA Backlogs—Myths vs. Reality*).

[45] Backlog data for 2005 were collected as a part of the Bureau of Justice Statistic's Census of Publicly Funded Forensic Crime Laboratories (see Matthew R. Durose, *Census of Publicly Funded Forensic Crime Laboratories, 2005*, NCJ 222181, July 2008, http://bjs.ojp.usdoj.gov/content/pub/pdf/cpffcl05.pdf). Data for 2007 were collected as a part of a NIJ funded study of DNA backlogs (see Lisa Hurst and Kevin Lothridge, "2007 DNA Evidence and Offender Measurement Analysis: DNA Backlogs, Capacity and Funding," NCJ 230328, January 2010, http://www.ncjrs.gov/ pdffiles1/nij/grants/230328.pdf). Data for 2008 were reported by applicants for NIJ's FY2009 DNA Backlog Reduction Program grant solicitation. Data for 2009 were reported by applicants for NIJ's FY2010 DNA Backlog Reduction Program. Ibid., p. 3.

[46] Ibid., p. 4.

[47] Ibid.

[48] Ibid., p. 1.

[49] Ibid., p. 7.

[50] Ibid., p. 8.

[51] Ibid., p. 2.

[52] Ibid.

[53] Kevin J. Strom, Jeri Ropero-Miller, and Shelton Jones et al., *The 2007 Survey of Law Enforcement Forensic Evidence Processing*, U.S. Department of Justice, Office of Justice

Programs, National Institute of Justice, Washington, DC, October 2009, pp. 3-2, http://www.ncjrs.gov/pdffiles1/nij/grants

[54] Ibid.

[55] Ibid., p. 3-7.

[56] Ibid., p. 3-6.

[57] Lisa Hurst and Kevin Lothridge, *2007 DNA Evidence and Offender Analysis Measurement: DNA Backlogs, Capacity and Funding*, Final Report to National Institute of Justice Grant 2006-MU-BX-K002, Washington, DC, January 2010, p. 8, http://www.ncjrs.gov/pdffiles1 /nij/grants/230328.pdf (hereinafter, *2007 DNA Evidence and Offender Analysis Measurement*).

[58] Ibid.

[59] Ibid., p. 12.

[60] Ibid.

[61] CBS News conducted a five month investigation into the backlog of sexual assault evidence collection kits. The investigation collected data on the number of backlogged kits in 24 cities and states. CBS News reports that there are more than 20,000 sexual assault evidence collection kits that were never sent to crime laboratories and another 6,000 kits from cases that are under active investigation, but are still waiting to be tested. The results of CBS News' investigation are available online at http://www.cbsnews.com/stories/2009/11/10 /cbsnews_investigates/ main5605770.shtml?tag=contentMain;contentBody.

[62] Nancy Ritter, "Solving the Problem of Untested Evidence in Sexual Assaults," *NIJ Journal*, no. 267 (Winter 2010), p. 18.

[63] Ibid., p. 19.

[64] Armen Keteyian, "Untested Rape Kits Lead to More Crimes," *CBS News*, November 10, 2009, http://www.cbsnews.com/stories/2009/11/10/cbsnews_investigates/main5603492.shtml.

[65] Rape, Abuse and Incest National Network (RAINN), *What is a Rape Kit*, http://www.rainn.org/get-information/ sexual-assault-recovery/rape-kit (hereinafter, *What is a Rape Kit*).

[66] U.S. Department of Justice, Office on Violence Against Women, *A National Protocol for Sexual Assault Medical Forensic Examinations*, NCJ 228119, April 2013, p. 7, https://www.ncjrs.gov/pdffiles1/ovw/241903.pdf (hereinafter, *A National Protocol for Sexual Assault Medical Forensic Examinations*).

[67] *What is a Rape Kit.*

[68] Ibid.

[69] Ibid.

[70] Angela Wu, "Will Rape Kit Testing Laws Help Clear Cases?," *Newsweek*, July 26, 2010, http://www.newsweek.com/will-rape (hereinafter, "Will Rape Kit Testing Laws Help Clear Cases?").

[71] Human Rights Watch, *Testing Justice: The Rape Kit Backlog in Los Angeles City and County*, 1-56432-461-3, New York, NY, March 2009, p. 22, http://www.hrw.org/sites/default /files/reports/rapekit0309webwcover.pdf.

[72] U.S. Department of Justice, Office of Justice Programs, National Institute of Justice, *Untested Sexual Assault Evidence in Law Enforcement Custody*, http://www.nij.gov/topics/forensics /lab-operations/evidence-backlogs/lawenforcement-sexual-assault.htm.

[73] Department of Justice, Office on Violence Against Women, *Eliminating the Rape Kit Backlog: A Roundtable to Explore a Victim-centered Approach*, Washington , DC, May 10, 2010, p. 15, http://www.ovw.usdoj.gov/docs/rape-

[74] Dan Cantillon, Kathy Kopiec, and Heather Clawson, *Evaluation of the Impact of the Forensic Casework DNA Backlog Reduction Program*, ICF International, Fairfax, VA, February 2009, p. 10, http://www.ncjrs.gov/pdffiles1/nij/ grants/225803.pdf (hereinafter, *Evaluation of the Impact of the Forensic Casework DNA Backlog Reduction Program*").

[75] Ibid., p. 11.

[76] Ibid.

[77] Ibid., p. 10.

[78] Ibid., p. 11.

[79] Ibid., p. 14.

[80] *Fundamentals of Forensic DNA Typing*, p. 275.

[81] Ibid.

[82] Ibid.

[83] The FBI permits forensic profiles with 10 of the 13 CODIS loci to be uploaded into the NDIS for searching against the offender and arrestee indexes. CODIS FAQs.

[84] David Lazer, *Searching the Family Tree for Suspects: Ethical and Implementation Issues in the Familial Searching of DNA Databases*, A. Alfred Taubman Center for State and Local Government, Cambridge, MA, March 2008, p. 1, http://www.hks.harvard.edu/var/ezp_site /storage lazer_final.pdf (hereinafter, Lazer, *Searching the Family Tree for Suspects*).

[85] Natalie Ram, *DNA Confidential: State Law Enforcement Policies for Genetic Databases Lack Transparency*, Science Progress, October 2009, p. 2, http://www.scienceprogress.org/2009 /11/dna-confidential/.

[86] Ibid., p. 1.

[87] Ibid., p. 3.

[88] Greely, Riordan, Garrison et al., "Family Ties," p. 251.

[89] Ibid., p. 252.

[90] Ibid.

[91] Ibid., p. 253.

[92] Ibid., p. 252.

[93] Ellen Nakashima, "From DNA of Family, a Tool to Make Arrests," *The Washington Post*, April 21, 2008.

[94] The FBI defines a "partial match" as a match between two single source profiles (i.e., offender profiles and forensic profiles that contain DNA from one perpetrator) having at least one allele in common at each locus. U.S. Department of Justice, Federal Bureau of Investigation, "Interim Plan for the Release of Information In the Event of a 'Partial Match' at NDIS," Bulletin #BT072006, July 20, 2006, http://www.bioforensics.com/conference08 /Familial_Searches/ CODIS_Bulletin.pdf.

[95] Sonia M. Suter, "All in the Family: Privacy and DNA Familial Searching," *Harvard Journal of Law and Technology*, vol. 23, no. 2 (Spring 2010), p. 324 (hereinafter, Suter, "All in the Family").

[96] 42 U.S.C. §14131(a)(2).

[97] The most recent QAS took effect on September 1, 2011.

[98] 42 U.S.C. §14131(a)(3).

[99] Ibid.

[100] 42 U.S.C. §14133(a)(1)(A).

[101] CODIS FAQs.

[102] Ibid.

[103] 42 U.S.C. §14132(a).

[104] Under the Violent Crime Control and Law Enforcement Act of 1994 (P.L. 103-322), the NDIS was only to include analyses of DNA samples collected from (1) individuals convicted of crimes, (2) crime scenes, and (3) unidentified human remains. The Justice for All Act of 2004 (P.L. 108-405) amended the authorizing legislation for the NDIS to allow analyses of DNA samples collected from persons who have been charged in an indictment or information with a crime and other persons whose DNA samples are collected under applicable legal authorities to be included in the NDIS, provided that profiles from arrestees who have not been charged with a crime and samples that are voluntarily submitted solely for elimination purposes are not included in the NDIS. The Violence Against Women and Department of Justice Reauthorization Act of 2005 (P.L. 109-162) amended the authorizing legislation for the NDIS to allow analyses of samples collected from arrestees to be included in the NDIS.

[105] According to the FBI, the American Society of Crime Laboratory Directors/Laboratory Accreditation Board (ASCLD/LAB) and Forensic Quality Services, Inc. (FQS) meet the definition specified at 42 U.S.C. §14132(b)(2)(A) for an accrediting organization. CODIS FAQs.

[106] 42 U.S.C. §14132(b).

[107] 42 U.S.C. §14132(d)(1)(A)(i).

[108] 42 U.S.C. §14132(d)(1)(A)(ii).

[109] 42 U.S.C. §14132(d)(2)(A)(i).

[110] 10 U.S.C. §1565(e).

[111] 42 U.S.C. §14135a(a)(1)(A).

[112] The DNA Analysis Backlog Elimination Act of 2000 (P.L. 106-546) required BOP and U.S. probation offices to collect DNA samples from anyone in their custody who was convicted of qualifying federal offenses. The act defined a "qualifying federal offense" as murder, voluntary manslaughter, or other offenses relating to homicide; an offense relating to sexual abuse, sexual exploitation or other abuse of children, or transportation for illegal sexual activity; an offense relating to peonage or slavery; kidnapping; an offense relating to robbery or burglary; any offense committed in Indian country relating to murder, manslaughter, kidnapping, maiming, a felony sexual abuse offense, incest, arson, robbery, or burglary; or any attempt or conspiracy to commit any of these crimes. The Uniting and Strengthening America by Providing Appropriate Tools Required to Intercept and Obstruct Terrorism (USA PATRIOT) Act of 2001 (P.L. 107-56) expanded the definition of "qualifying federal offense" to include crimes of terrorism, crimes of violence, or any attempt or conspiracy to commit either crime. The Justice for All Act of 2004 (P.L. 108-405) amended the definition of "qualifying federal offense" to include any felony, sexual abuse offense, crime of violence, or attempt or conspiracy to commit any of these crimes. The Violence Against Women and Department of Justice Reauthorization Act of 2005 (P.L. 109-162) authorized DOJ to collect DNA samples from arrestees and non-citizens who are detained under the authority of the United States. The Adam Walsh Child Protection and Safety Act of 2006 (P.L. 109-248) authorized DOJ to also collect DNA samples from individuals facing charges in addition to those who have been arrested or convicted.

[113] As defined at 18 U.S.C. §16.

[114] 42 U.S.C. §14135a(a)(1)(B).

[115] 42 U.S.C. §14135a(a)(2).

[116] 42 U.S.C. §14135a(b).

[117] 42 U.S.C. §14135b(a)(1).

[118] 42 U.S.C. §14135b(a)(2).

[119] 42 U.S.C. §14135b(d).

[120] 42 U.S.C. §14135b(b). The following are considered qualifying offenses under the D.C. Code: (1) any felony; (2) any offense for which the penalty is greater than one year imprisonment; (3) lewd, indecent, or obscene acts knowingly committed in the presence of a child under 16 years of age (D.C. Code §22-1312(b)); (4) certain obscene activities involving minors (D.C. Code §22-2201); (5) sexual performances using a minor (D.C. Code §22-3102); (6) misdemeanor sexual abuse (D.C. Code §22-3006); (7) misdemeanor sexual abuse of child or a minor (D.C. Code §22- 3010.01); or (8) any attempt or conspiracy to commit any of these crimes. D.C. Code §22-4151.

[121] 10 U.S.C. §1565(a)(1).

[122] The requirement to collect DNA samples for people convicted of certain offenses under the Uniform Code of Military Justice is separate from the DNA samples the Department of Defense collects to aid in the identification of human remains.

[123] 10 U.S.C. §1565(b).

[124] 18 U.S.C. §3600(a).

[125] There is a rebuttable presumption of timeliness if the motion is made within 60 months of the enactment of the Justice for All Act of 2004 (October 30, 2004) or within 36 months of conviction, whichever comes later. The presumption of timeliness may be rebutted upon a showing that the applicant's motion for DNA testing is based solely upon information used in a previously denied motion or of clear and convincing evidence that the applicant's filing is done solely to cause delay or harass. For any motion that is not made within 60 months of the enactment of the Justice for All Act of 2004 or within 36 months of conviction, there is a rebuttable presumption against timeliness. The presumption against timeliness can be rebutted upon the court's finding (1) that the applicant was or is incompetent and such incompetence substantially contributed to the delay in the applicant's motion for a DNA test; (2) the evidence to be tested is newly discovered DNA evidence; (3) that the applicant's motion is not based solely upon the applicant's own assertion of innocence and, after considering all relevant facts and circumstances surrounding the motion, a denial would result in a manifest injustice; or (4) upon good cause shown. 18 U.S.C. §3600(a)(10)(B).

[126] 18 U.S.C. §3600(c)(1).

[127] 18 U.S.C. §3600(c)(2).

[128] 18 U.S.C. §3600(c)(3).

[129] 18 U.S.C. §3600(e)(2).

[130] 18 U.S.C. §3600(e)(3)(A).

[131] 18 U.S.C. §3600(e)(3)(B).

[132] 18 U.S.C. §3600(e)(3)(C).

[133] 18 U.S.C. §3600(f)(1).

[134] Each prisoner serving a term of imprisonment of more than one year, but not prisoners serving a life sentence, can receive a good time credit of up to 54 days per year to count toward serving the sentence. The amount of the credit is subject to the determination of BOP. 18 U.S.C. §3624(b).

[135] 18 U.S.C. §3600(f)(2).

[136] 18 U.S.C. §3600(f)(3).

[137] 18 U.S.C. §3600(g)(1).

[138] 18 U.S.C. §3600(g)(2).

[139] 18 U.S.C. §3600A(a).

[140] "Biological evidence" is defined as a sexual assault forensic examination kit, or semen, blood, saliva, hair, skin tissue, or other identified biological material. 18 U.S.C. §3600A(b).

[141] 18 U.S.C. §3600A(c).

[142] The DNA Backlog Elimination Act of 2000 (P.L. 106-546) authorized grants to increase the capacity of state and local government laboratories to conduct DNA analysis of biological samples from crime scenes.

[143] On March 11, 2003, President George W. Bush announced his DNA Initiative, "Advancing Justice Through DNA Technology," which provided "funds, training, and assistance to ensure that DNA technology reaches its full potential to solve crimes, protect the innocent, and identify missing persons." From FY2004 to FY2007, Congress appropriated funding for the President's DNA initiative, although the initiative was not authorized in statute.

[144] U.S. Congress, House Committee on Appropriations, Subcommittee on Science, The Departments of State, Justice, and Commerce, and Related Agencies, *Making Appropriations for Science, the Departments of State, Justice, Commerce and Related Agencies for the Fiscal Year Ending September 30, 2006, and for Other Purposes*, Report to Accompany H.R. 2862, 109th Cong., 1st sess., November 7, 2005, H.Rept. 109-272 (Washington: GPO, 2005), p. 121.

[145] See P.L. 110-161, P.L. 111-8, P.L. 111-117, P.L. 112-55, P.L. 113-6, and P.L. 113-76.

[146] A breakdown of awards under each of these programs is available online at http://nij.gov/funding/

[147] Frederick R. Bieber, Charles H. Brenner, and David Lazer, "Finding Criminals Through DNA of Their Relatives," *Science*, vol. 312, no. 5778 (June 2, 2006), p. 1316 (hereinafter, Bieber, Brenner, and Lazer, "Finding Criminals Through the DNA of Their Relatives," p. 1316).

[148] Ibid.

[149] Ibid.

[150] Erin Murphy, "Relative Doubt: Familial Searches of DNA Databases," *Michigan Law Review*, vol. 109, no. 3 (December 2010), p. 306 (hereinafter, Murphy, "Relative Doubt").

[151] Ibid., p. 307.

[152] Suter, "All in the Family," p. 361.

[153] Greely, Riordan, Garrison et al., "Family Ties," p. 257.

[154] Epstein, "Genetic Surveillance," p. 171.

[155] Murphy, "Relative Doubt," p. 308.

[156] Ibid.

[157] Bieber, Brenner, and Lazer, "Finding Criminals Through the DNA of Their Relatives," p. 1316.

[158] Kimberly A. Wah, "A New Investigative Lead: Familial Searching as an Effective Crime-Fighting Tool," *Whittier Law Review*, vol. 29, no. 4 (Summer 2008), p. 976 (hereinafter, Wah, "A New Investigative Lead").

[159] Y-chromosomes and mitochondrial DNA (mtDNA) are considered "lineage markers" because they are passed down from one generation to the next without changing (except for cases where they mutate). The Y-chromosome is only found in males. Paternal lineages can be traced using Y-chromosome markers because a father passes his Y-chromosome on to his son. Therefore, fathers and sons and brothers will share the same Y-chromosome (except for cases where the chromosome mutates). In contrast, mtDNA is only passed from a mother to her children, therefore all siblings with the same biological mother will share the same mtDNA (except for cases where the mtDNA mutates), as opposed to the Y-chromosome, which is only shared by male siblings. In addition, children will share mtDNA with maternal relatives. Therefore, mtDNA can be used to trace maternal lineage. John M.

Butler, *Forensic DNA Typing: Biology, Technology, and Genetics of STR Markers (2nd ed.)* (Burlington, MA: Elsevier Academic Press, 2005), pp. 201-204 and 247-249.

160 Murphy, "Relative Doubt," p. 300.

161 Suter, "All in the Family," pp. 368-370.

162 Ibid., p. 370.

163 Greely, Riordan, Garrison et al., "Family Ties," p. 259.

164 Suter, "All in the Family," p. 370.

165 Lazer, *Searching the Family Tree for Suspects*, p. 6.

166 Ibid., pp. 6-7.

167 Epstein, "Genetic Surveillance," p. 163.

168 Ibid., p. 165.

169 Jessica D. Gabel, "Probable Cause from Probable Bonds: A Genetic Tattle Tail Based on Familial DNA," *Hastings Women's Law Journal*, vol. 21, no. 1 (Winter 2010), p. 41 (hereinafter, Gabel, "Probable Cause from Probable Bonds").

170 Epstein, "Genetic Surveillance," p. 165.

171 Gabel, "Probable Cause from Probable Bonds," p. 42.

172 Suter, "All in the Family," p. 328.

173 Lazer, *Searching the Family Tree for Suspects*, p. 6.

174 U.S. Congress, House Committee on Appropriations, *Agriculture, Rural Development, Food and Drug Administration, and Related Agencies Programs for the Fiscal Year Ending September 30, 2012, and for Other Purposes*, Conference Report to Accompany H.R. 2112, 112th Cong., 1st sess., November 14, 2011, H.Rept. 112-284 (Washington: GPO, 2011), p. 238.

175 Ibid.

176 *2007 DNA Evidence and Offender Analysis Measurement*, p. 9.

177 Ibid.

178 Ibid., p. 13.

179 Matthew R. Durose, Kelly A. Walsh, and Andrea M. Burch, *Census of Publicly Funded Forensic Crime Laboratories, 2009*, U.S. Department of Justice, Office of Justice Programs, Bureau of Justice Statistics, NCJ 238252, Washington, DC, August 2012, p. 5, http://www.bjs.gov/content/pub/pdf/cpffcl09.pdf.

180 Ibid.

181 Ibid.

182 *Evaluation of the Impact of the Forensic Casework DNA Backlog Reduction Program*, p. 50.

183 Ibid.

184 *Making Sense of DNA Backlogs, 2010—Myths vs. Reality*, p. 8.

185 Ibid., p. 49.

186 Dr. Boschwitz is a vice president and executive officer of Orchid Cellmark, Inc., "one of the largest worldwide providers of human DNA testing." Testimony of Dr. Boschwitz, p. 81.

187 Ibid.

188 Ibid., pp. 82-83.

189 Ibid., p. 83.

190 *Melendez-Diaz v. Massachusetts*, 129 S.Ct. 2527 (2009).

191 Testimony of Dr. Boschwitz, p. 83.

192 Ibid.

193 Ibid., p. 84.

194 Ranajit Chakroborty and Jianye Ge, "Statistical Weight of a DNA Match in Cold-hit Cases," *Forensic Science Communications*, vol. 11, no. 3 (July 2009).

[195] 42 U.S.C. §14135(f).

[196] For more information on the JAG program, see CRS Report RS22416, *Edward Byrne Memorial Justice Assistance Grant (JAG) Program*, by Nathan James.

[197] Matthew R. Durose, Kelly A. Walsh, and Andrea M. Burch, *Census of Publicly Funded Forensic Crime Laboratories, 2009*, U.S. Department of Justice, Office of Justice Programs, Bureau of Justice Statistics, NCJ 238252, Washington, DC, August 2012, p. 11, http://www.bjs.gov/content/pub/pdf/cpffcl09.pdf.

[198] *A National Protocol for Sexual Assault Medical Forensic Examinations*, pp. 71-72.

[199] Ibid., p. 72.

[200] National Conference of State Legislatures, http://www.ncsl.org/research/civil-and-criminal-justice/dna-lawsdatabase.aspx.

[201] Matthew R. Durose, Kelly A. Walsh, and Andrea M. Burch, *Census of Publicly Funded Forensic Crime Laboratories, 2009*, U.S. Department of Justice, Office of Justice Programs, Bureau of Justice Statistics, NCJ 238252, Washington, DC, August 2012, p. 7, http://www.bjs.gov/content/pub/pdf/cpffcl09.pdf.

INDEX

D

E

F

G

H

I

J

K

L

M

N

O

P

Q

R

S

T

U

V

W